"This is the best book on the Federal Reserve ever written. An inside look at the Federal Reserve from an insider. Jim Kudlinski is not your typical Ph.D. He is a practitioner, a tough guy and a straight talker. This is a book for everyone, not just bankers and Fed alumni. This is a book for Main Street and Wall Street. Jim takes you places you have never been before. He accurately conveys what it is like to be at the most powerful financial institution on the planet. Alexander Hamilton would be proud."

—Raymond F. Hodgdon III
President, Enlightened Economics

"This is a colorful account of how the Fed really works. Kudlinski had an intimate vantage point from which to observe the personalities and events that have moved this remarkable organization forward. It is, after all, one of the very few agencies of the federal government that actually works. Clear, penetrating, interesting. I wholeheartedly recommend the book to the general reader as well as the professional student of the central bank."

—Ron Burke
Former President and CEO,
Bank Administration Institute

The Tarnished Fed

The Tarnished Fed

Behind Closed Doors: Forty
Years of Successes, Failures,
Mystique, and Humor

Jim Kudlinski

VANTAGE PRESS
New York

Copyright © 2010 by Jim Kudlinski

Published by Vantage Press, Inc.
419 Park Ave. South, New York, NY 10016

Manufactured in the United States of America
ISBN: 978-0-533-16318-2

Library of Congress Catalog Card No: 2009911539

0 9 8 7 6 5 4 3 2 1

To
Mr. and Mrs. Alois A. Kudlinski

and

Dr. and Mrs. Roland T. Rohwer

and to my grandchildren:
Chelsea Prim
"RJ" Prim
Evan Kudlinski
Maggie Kudlinski
Sydney Kudlinski
Zach Kudlinski
Roland Kudlinski
Drew Kudlinski
Jake Kudlinski
Lucy Kudlinski
Abbey Crews
Courtney Crews

Contents

Acknowledgments

I am thankful for the cooperation of the officers in the Division of Reserve Bank Operations and Payment Systems, Board of Governors of the Federal Reserve System, and their provision of information and updates on the Fed: Louise Roseman, Jeffrey Marquardt, Paul Bettge, Kenneth Buckley, Dorothy La Chapelle, Jack Walton, Jeff Stehm, Gregory Evans, Lisa Hoskins, and Michael Lambert.

Many thanks to Catherine Tunis, assistant chief librarian in the research library at the Board of Governors in Washington D.C. Her responses to my inquiries were always prompt and complete.

Thanks to Jim Williams, former executive at the Office of Thrift Supervision and the Resolution Trust Corporation, for his recollections about the S&L crisis, and for his thorough review of my book and suggestions.

Thanks to my children and their spouses for their interest, reviews, suggestions, and encouragement: John and Ruth, Ted and Sherri, Jim and Susie, Mary and Brian, and Kathy and Rick. Special thanks to my oldest son, John—this book was his original idea and his suggestions throughout its writing were invaluable—and to Kathy, Mary, and Chelsea for doing the word processing. They were terrific. Brian Crews kept my old computer working on many occasions when I thought I had inadvertently "lost" the book because of technical problems. And his contributions on the book were insightful.

I very much appreciate the review of and comments on the book by Francis Prendergast, my football coach at Kelly and a legend in high school football in Chicago. Never has a quarterback had a better coach and mentor.

Thanks to my brother Jerry, Paula, Victoria, and to Judd and Kathryn Sackheim, Mary Lemek, and to Betty Kudlinski, Barbara Lawrence and Doug and Dolly Layman for their encouragement, interest, support, and editorial comments.

Joyce Lohrentz, Joanne Grider, Dr. Hal Bayne, Jim Vermette, Bob Rauth, Leroy Gall, and Jerry Zubek were encouraging and supportive, as they have been since I have known them.

But most of all, I remain indebted to my wife Ginny—not just for her encouragement and patience in my efforts to complete this book, but for everything she has done for me to enable me to be successful in life. The day I married her 48 years ago, I felt like I had won the lottery. I still do.

Thank you one and all. You made this book fun to write.

Preface

Nora worked in the wire transfer department of the Chicago Fed. She transcribed wire instructions received via telephone from any of the 3,200 commercial banks located in the Seventh District, and was one of about 250 Fed people assigned this task. Banks desiring to wire funds would call the Fed and be placed in a telephone queue that was serviced on a first-in, first-answered basis.

She pressed the button to connect to the next caller in the queue, who identified himself as David. He said he had wire instructions, and proceeded to give her the spelling of his last name, his bank's name and ABA number, the receiving bank's name and ABA number, the name and account number of the corporation to which funds were being wired at the receiving bank, and the dollar amount—which was $15 million.

Nora dutifully transcribed the data on to the proper form as David recited the information, Then she said, "The code, please." After a pause, David responded with, "Ah . . . code?"

Nora sensed that he probably was not aware of the new procedures instituted recently, so she said, "Check with your supervisor, I'll wait on the line." She heard a click, and shortly thereafter, realized that a disconnection occurred.

She retrieved his bank's wire-department phone number from her rolodex file and called, asking for him. When she was connected, he sounded strangely different. He told her he knew nothing about a $15 million wire. After ascertaining that he was certain he did not initiate such a wire request, she hung up and decided to notify her supervisor, who in turn reported the incident to the officers in charge of wire operations at the Chicago Fed.

The law enforcement authorities were called in to investigate. They ultimately determined, among other matters, that the wire request came from a pay phone in the state prison in Joliet, Illinois.

By the 1970s the Fed's domestic and international payment systems were antiquated, its bank and branch buildings no longer serviceable, and its technology out dated. This was accompanied by a period of record-setting interest rate levels in this country and abroad, which added to the Fed's concerns. The story of how the Fed coped with these, thereby avoiding a myriad of problems, including criminal penetration of their operations, sheds new light on what goes on behind the closed doors of the most powerful central bank in the world.

This situation became the catalyst for revolutionary changes inside the Fed, which began in the 1970s, continued in the 1980s, intensified in the 1990s, and are still going on. All were done—like most things by the Fed—in a low-key manner and without fanfare. All were funded by their enormous profitability, which enables them to purchase talent and technology as required to achieve success, and is the engine that makes everything else go inside our central bank. Surprisingly, the importance of such self-funding to the Fed has gone virtually unnoticed for decades.

Since the Fed officers are free to act without political constraint or interference, which makes them unique among our government and pseudo-government organizations, how well have they handled the trust empowered to them? And not just the monetary-policy portion, but all of their responsibilities.

At the time Alan Greenspan resigned the Fed chairmanship in early 2006, accolades were heard from all over the planet, praising his direction of our nation's monetary policy. He conducted these in an almost flawless manner throughout his eighteen years as "maestro" of the Fed. His legacy as the greatest of all Fed chairmen seemed assured.

That is, until the subprime mortgage mess surfaced causing lock-up of our capital markets and widespread problems in our economy which eventually globalized. When it became known that the Fed did not fulfill it's supervisory and regulatory responsibilities over the mortgage banking industry, which Congress assigned to Greenspan's Fed in the mid-1990s—thus enabling mortgage bankers and Wall Street to perpetrate the ill-conceived, corrosive, and highly toxic subprime mortgage scheme upon us all—the touting of Greenspan's work as Fed chairman abruptly terminated. Those "best of all Fed chairmen" voices ceased and have not been heard from since.

And Ben Bernanke's legacy also has been discolored by the same brush. It took until May of 2008 for Bernanke's Fed to propose more stringent regulatory rules over the mortgage banking industry. And these may be too little, and certainly are too late.

Conventional wisdom as reported in the financial press has attributed the subprime mess to, among other matters, the Fed being "asleep at the switch," which they were, by Greenspan's admission. This most recent regulatory lapse is indeed disturbing, especially when considered in conjunction with the failure of the S&L industry over two decades ago. That failure cost the taxpayers $124 billion in bailout costs and was the result of poor public policy and incompetent thrift management and regulation, although the Fed was an accomplice.

But in the subprime mess, the Fed was much more than just an accomplice. To date, over $10 trillion in public funds have been committed to ameliorate the problems caused by this debacle. And we are still mired in its tentacles.

But if the truth be known, even if the Fed had done its job and was aware, day-by-day, of what was occurring in the mortgage banking industry from 2003 to early 2007, it is questionable whether they would have taken the action necessary to avert the subprime problem. Why? For the same reason that Congress was unwilling to avert the S&L debacle. The political cost was unacceptable. The similarities between these two nationwide financial catastrophes provide important lessons to which we should all be attentive.

This book consists of twelve chapters. Chapters 1–4 take the reader inside our central bank, into its headquarters, offices, meeting rooms, operations, and unusual decision-making structure. Chapters 5–8 take the reader inside the Fed revolution, about which little is known to the general public. In chapters 9–12, the reader gets to be a "fly on the wall" inside the offices of our contemporary Fed chairmen. These include Burns, Miller, Volcker, Greenspan, and Bernanke. I worked daily with three of these men, and observed all of their chairmanships as only a former Fed executive could do whose position required him to perform and interact as an "insider" at the focus of power in this secretive bureaucratic organization.

Chapters 9–12 provides the unvarnished truth about the S&L crisis and the subprime mess and exposes those to blame. With regard to our most recent financial catastrophe, there are many culprits, including the Fed, the rating agencies, Congress, predatory lenders, clueless as well as greedy borrowers, other financial regulators, and, of course, CEOs of some of our major financial organizations who loaded up their balance sheets with toxic assets in the pursuit of profits and excess compensatory rewards that almost pushed our nation over the edge.

But inside the Fed, the key culprit—besides Greenspan, the man in charge—was Timothy Geithner, then president of the New York Fed Bank and now treasury secretary in the Obama Administration. The subprime mess occurred right in Timothy's "backyard," better known as Wall Street, while he slept at his desk at the New York Fed. The subprime problem simmered and ultimately boiled over during a period of three to four years, and not one person at the New York Fed, or at the Board of Governors in Washington, D.C., had even a clue that something was amiss. It is not often that all levels of risk management in our financial industry fail simultaneously, but in this case it did.

President Obama's Administration has proposed regulatory reform intended to prevent the recurrence of a subprime-type problem. But overlooked in this regulatory reform are some required basic changes within the Fed, and in the practices of our executive and legislative branches, which are essential if the Fed and our nation are to avoid embarrassment in the future.

There are many humorous incidents in this book, which involve VIPs from banking, business, Congress, and the presidential administrations interspersed throughout, several Fed heroes, some known and others not well known, and descriptions of major and costly errors and of the greedy who attempted personal gain at public expense. Included are 65 anecdotes describing the most interesting and entertaining of my experiences in the Fed that take the reader to places "never before seen."

All things reported in this book actually occurred. The time period covered is 1970 to the present.

What is discussed in this book has never been in print before. So let's start with explaining why.

The Tarnished Fed

1

A Fed Within the Fed

Most everyone is aware of the "repackaging" that occurs when, for example, an entertainer, actor, or actress begins achieving stardom. The same applies to an athlete, a promising political figure, model, etc. After the marketing and publicity people complete their work, what remains hardly resembles the person they started with. But underneath that façade, inside where it counts, very little, if anything about the individual has really changed.

Organizations also have undergone "image" changes, including their key executives. Almost always, these are by design and are carefully crafted. On very rare occasions, however, an impetus can build up, which if left unabated, becomes the "conventional wisdom"—and presto, society has created a perception of an organization, and even of its key executives, that does not reflect reality. That is exactly what happened with the Fed, and thus one of the reasons for this book.

From the time that authors first started writing books about the Fed (and there currently are 241 of these on library shelves, give or take a few), their focus has been on monetary policy. Our national news media, including newspapers, radio, TV, and the Internet, have reported on monetary policy and ignored everything else the Fed does. Only the banking journalists have been somewhat attentive in their reporting of the overall responsibilities of the Fed.

Perhaps the national media have been somewhat misled by the Fed itself in this direction. Traditionally, their chairmen—starting at least with Arthur Burns in 1970 and continuing through to Alan Greenspan in 2006—have been less than forthcoming in their pronouncements on monetary policy and have rarely, if ever, reported on any of the other activities of our central bank.

Our press and media also have had a tendency to create Fed legends, namely, FOMC chairmen, including Burns, Volcker, Greenspan; and, earlier, Eccles and Martin. But they create them for the wrong reasons.

The "FOMC," or Federal Open Market Committee, is the organization inside the Fed charged with conducting our nation's monetary policy. What you may not know, however, is that the FOMC is a "Fed within the Fed" and a "compartmented" area inside our central bank. What does this mean? Exactly what it means in government and military service when you have a security clearance.

In the Fed, only those personnel who are part of the FOMC organization, including the twelve voting members, seven Fed presidents, and their FOMC support staff have access to FOMC data, information, deliberations, and to meetings where decisions are made. Others are totally excluded, and there is zero tolerance in the Fed for any violations.

All other Fed personnel learn of FOMC decisions at the same time the entire market is informed. FOMC phone lines and data links are encrypted to preclude any unauthorized access to their deliberations and decisions. The reason for such stringent security is that a person could profit substantially by having access to FOMC decisions, prior to their becoming known to the market, to the detriment of the participants.

All of the press and media reports on monetary policy actually are reports on the activities of the "Fed within the Fed." Occasionally reporters, analysts, and commentators become enamored with some of the players and this leads to exaggerations—particularly with regard to the prowess of FOMC chairmen (who also are Fed chairmen) and their abilities to discern from the data what no other FOMC members or staff could do on their own. The image that is created is of an FOMC chairman, particularly one such as Greenspan, folding the sheets of data and putting these into his back pocket, entering his office to study and contemplate, and emerging with the answer that everyone missed, thus saving the day.

That's not how things happen. The FOMC has 1,400 staffers that daily follow each and every market segment in the economy. They are experts in their areas of specialization.

For example, when I was with the Federal Reserve Board in Washington, D.C., I tried to hire one of these into my division, an economist by the name of Dave Seiders. He was the Fed's residential mortgage loan market expert. He declined what would have been a sizable promotion if he had joined my division and he remained with the monetary policy staff as its expert in that market. Subsequently, he left the Fed and is now the chief economist for the National Home Builders Association, as an expert in the residential mortgage industry, and is nationally known today.

And there are other, more senior economic advisors in the Fed that interpret what the data mean. There are also the FOMC voting members and Fed Bank presidents and their support staffs who do likewise. FOMC decisions are the culmination of this process. There are no "lone rangers" to be "deified." These exist only as image creations of the press and media—who apparently are proponents of tennis great Andre Agassi's phrase, "Image is everything."

The Fed has been flaunted as a very powerful organization—which it is. But that power has been attributed solely to the FOMC and its monetary policy activities.

If you removed the FOMC from inside the Fed, would you still have as powerful and effective a monetary policy in our nation? Would you still have as powerful a Fed?

This move was proposed and debated in the banking industry and among the legislators at the time Congress passed the Monetary Control Act of 1980, which opened access to Fed services to all financial institutions and required the Fed to price for its services, among other matters.

The large banks in our country were lining up to make

3

claim to the Fed's payments-mechanism functions, which are a significant part of the other things—besides monetary policy—that it does. Two arguments shot down the big banks in their quest to take over these functions. First, these are so critical to our society and economy and to maintaining financial leadership in the world, that we could not risk disruption—even if such were a minimal risk—in the transition to and operation of the Fed's payments-mechanism functions in the private sector. And secondly, the Fed's implementation of our nation's monetary policy relies heavily upon these other functions. The point to be made is that if you fragment the Fed, like our news media has done in its reporting, the result would be a greatly diminished organization in terms of power, influence, prestige, and capability. This will become clear to you as you proceed through this book. Also, you will understand the tremendous advantage afforded the FOMC by its insertion inside of the Fed and its reliance upon the other things that the Fed does when implementing our nation's monetary policy. The subprime mess already has shown us what can happen to our nation and to the Fed's reputation and that of its chairman if it fails in the performance of its "other" responsibilities. This will become even more critical in the future, especially if the Fed is assigned additional responsibilities, as is currently contemplated in President Obama's regulatory reform proposals.

For now, however, let's focus on the *four sources* of the Fed's power—which has no equal, nor even a runner-up, in the national and international financial markets—and on where such power resides in our "banker's bank."

2

Profitability and Power

Four Sources of Fed Power

The Fed is by far the most unusual and powerful of any of our federal government-type organizations. It is enormously profitable—which alone differentiates it from all others. From 1970 through 2005, for example, its total earnings were $651 billion. How were these earnings used?

The Fed required $50 billion for its expenses; $8 billion was needed to manufacture our currency; $7 billion was paid as dividends to the owners of Federal Reserve stock; $570 billion was given to the U.S. Treasury; and $16 billion was transferred to the Fed's surplus account, of which $13 billion remains, the majority of the difference having been given to the Treasury in 2000. Let's put these numbers in better perspective.

That same year, the Fed's earnings were $30.7 billion. By comparison, Exxon, our nation's largest firm, earned $36.13 billion, and Microsoft, a company with one of the largest publicly held stocks in the nation, earned $12.25 billion. The Fed's earnings were applied as follows: $3.16 billion was required for its operating expenses; $477 million was paid for the manufacture of our nation's money; $781 million provided dividends to the owners of Federal Reserve stock; $21.5 billion was given to the U.S. Treasury; $1.27 billion was transferred to the Fed's surplus account; and another $3.58 billion was required for, among other things, a $2.7 billion loss on foreign exchange transactions in which the Fed participates from time to time.

The great majority of these earnings came from interest payments on the huge portfolio of government securities that the Fed owns and manipulates in the market in conducting monetary policy. At the end of 2005, this portfolio consisted of $744 billion of U.S. Treasury bills, notes, and bonds. The other sources of its earnings were the $1.3 billion in fees for services provided. Financial depository institutions in our nation paid the Fed $901 million for services received, and the Fed was reimbursed $396 million for services received by the Federal government, primarily the U.S. Treasury.

This large annual income stream for the Fed enables it to "buy" as much talent and technology as it requires to fund its needs, including the revolutionary changes that have occurred since the 1970's which will be discussed later in this book. No other government or pseudo-governmental organization is equipped with such an unlimited "checkbook." The Fed's profitability, and its total independence in determining how such funds will be used, are responsible, in large measure, for the "power" that it wields nationally as well as internationally. These earnings are the "engine" that makes everything else go inside the Fed. Such self-funding greatly facilitates preservation of its political independence.

The Fed is solely responsible for the conduct of monetary policy in our country, the largest economy in the world. We account for one-third of the world's GDP. The Fed determines our price of money, better known as interest rates, and this has a major bearing on the price of money throughout the world's economies.

The Fed controls and regulates our nation's payments mechanism—through which our money, and that of the world's, moves in the settlement of domestic and international business and government transactions. It also is the operator of the nationwide infrastructure of the payments mechanism, without which our economic leadership in the world would be in jeopardy.

Further, the Fed supervises and regulates much of the banking industry, and grants approval for "change of control" upon sales and acquisitions of banks by bank holding companies, which "house" approximately 87 percent of the banking assets in our nation.

The Fed also supervises and regulates our largest banks that are "members" of the Federal Reserve System. It would be very difficult for any money center or regional bank to function without being a member of the Fed. At the end of 2005, for example, there were 7,844 commercial banks in operation, of which 2,698 were Fed members. But these member banks owned and operated 52,639 banking offices of the total of 75,731 in operation, and "housed" 76 percent of our nation's deposits.

Because of its profitability, its monetary-policy monopoly, payments-mechanism control and operation, and banking supervision and regulation, it is an enormously powerful organization. Most of the nations in the world have a central bank, but none of these come even close to the power wielded by the Fed in our economy, and in the world.

The Fed's nationwide organization in 2005 included 22,000 employees, of which 2,000 worked at the Board of Governors offices in Washington D.C., which is the "headquarters" of the Fed, and the remainder worked at twelve Federal Reserve Banks, twenty-five branches, and a handful of sundry offices—all spread throughout the United States. Employment has hovered close to this number ever since, but is likely to rise as the Fed assumes more responsibilities contemplated in the financial regulatory reform.

Chart 1 shows the location of the Fed's nationwide facilities. There is only one state that has two Federal Reserve Banks within—Missouri, which has a bank in Kansas City and another in St. Louis. Senator Carter Glass, who was instrumental in the passage of the Federal Reserve Act, which established the Federal Reserve System, was from the state of Missouri. He took care of his constituents by giving them two Fed banks. If the Federal Reserve System were established today, it would not look like that shown in Chart 1. The concentration of economic and banking activity today is different from

Chart 1

Federal Reserve Banks, Branches, and Districts

Federal Reserve Bank of Boston

Fed District 1

Federal Reserve Bank of New York
    Branch: Buffalo, New York

Fed District 2

Federal Reserve Bank of Philadelphia

Fed District 3

Federal Reserve Bank of Cleveland
    Branches: Cincinnati, Ohio
           Pittsburgh, Pennsylvania

Fed District 4

Federal Reserve Bank of Richmond
    Branches: Baltimore, Maryland
           Charlotte, North Carolina

Fed District 5

Federal Reserve Bank of Atlanta
    Branches: Birmingham, Alabama
           Jacksonville, Florida
           Miami, Florida
           Nashville, Tennessee New
           Orleans, Louisiana

Fed District 6

Federal Reserve Bank of Chicago
    Branch: Detroit, Michigan

Fed District 7

Federal Reserve Bank of St Louis
    Branches: Little Rock, Arkansas
           Louisville, Kentucky
           Memphis, Tennessee

Fed District 8

Federal Reserve Bank of Minneapolis
    Branch: Helena, Montana

Fed District 9

Federal Reserve Bank of Kansas City
    Branches: Denver, Colorado
           Oklahoma City,
           Oklahoma Omaha,
           Nebraska

Fed District 10

Federal Reserve Bank of Dallas
    Branches: El Paso, Texas
           Houston,   Texas
           San Antonio, Texas

Fed District 11

Federal Reserve Bank of San Francisco
    Branches: Los Angeles, California
           Portland, Oregon Salt Lake
           City, Utah Seattle,
           Washington

Fed District 12

8

what it was then, and today's technology could easily support less physical structures.

The Fed chairman is best known as the second most powerful man in our country, right behind our president. The national news reporting media describes him as the "key maker of our monetary policy." Whenever the Fed takes action in an attempt to move interest rates up or down—or is contemplating doing so—the media reports it to you, and also lets you know whenever its chairman reports on anything to the Congress, which is usually about the FOMC's monetary-policy activities or economic matters affecting the nation. The media also lets you know when the Fed fouls up on any of its responsibilities that have national or worldwide significance. But by then it is usually too late as the horse is already out of the barn (e.g., as in the subprime problem).

That's the focus of the national media coverage of the Fed, and the extent of general public knowledge of our central bank. This is unfortunate, because, based upon its annual expenditures, monetary policy represents only about 17 percent of what the Fed actually does, and the other 83 percent has remained essentially hidden behind closed doors throughout its history and is exposed only when problems materialize. (Total Fed operating expenses in 2005 for example, were $3.16 billion, of which $521.2 million was required to support its monetary policy activities.) Why has this occurred? For three reasons.

First, the media focuses on monetary policy and therefore may not be as knowledgeable as it should be about the other things the Fed does.

Second, the Fed does not actively seek publicity nor is it very forthcoming about anything it does. When it is required to make a public utterance, it usually does so in obfuscated language that has become known as "Fed-eez." For example, you and I would say, "Too many cooks spoil the broth." The "Fed-eez" translation might look like this: "Excessive amounts of culinary assistance, all other factors held constant, ultimately will result in diminishing returns from additional labor input, and reasonably may be expected to have a detrimental impact on the consomme."

The Fed is indeed most comfortable operating behind closed doors.

Third, and this is the rationale for its "close to the vest" tradition, the Fed jealously, closely, and carefully guards its unique and total political independence. In its view, the less that is known about it, the better.

All other Federal-government-type organizations are parts of the executive branch and get their directions from our president. Their budgets are approved by Congress and they must answer to the Congress for what they do, and don't do. As you know, whoever controls the "purse strings" is in control.

The Fed is not part of the executive branch. It is totally independent, approves its own budget, and answers to itself for what it has done, and has not done.

From time to time, Congress will ask for briefings from the Fed, and has an opportunity to chastise it for its actions, and to make suggestions. (Also, the Fed submits a printed annual report to the Congress, which is required by the Federal Reserve Act. This report summarizes the Fed's activities from the previous year.) The White House occasionally will lobby the Fed for certain actions. But neither can direct the Fed.

Anytime the Fed's political independence is threatened by anyone, including Congress or the White House, the Fed will bring out a defense that would make that of the Pittsburgh Steelers look grossly ineffective. I saw this defense firsthand and was part of it. The threat quickly dissipates. We will again see this defense in action as Bernanke and the Fed defend their turf against Congress's threatened audit of the Fed's monetary policy and other operations.

Banker's Bank

The Fed is our nation's central bank. The term "central bank" means "banker's bank," i.e., the Fed provides services to other banks and bank-like organizations, and to a very select and small grouping of others—such as securities dealers on Wall Street. This may go as far as "bailing" some out, such as occurred with Citibank, Bank of America, and other financial institutions, to prevent a collapse of our financial markets.

You, for example, cannot have an account with the Fed. Your bank, S&L, or credit union that provides you with financial services can.

In addition, the Fed provides banking services to Federal government organizations, and is the bank of the U.S. Treasury. The U.S. Treasury conducts all of its banking business through the Fed, including collecting payments, making disbursements, and delivering Social Security payments to retired recipients.

Power Inside the Fed

The final decision—making authority in the Fed for 17 percent of what it does—monetary policy—is the Federal Open Market Committee (FOMC). The FOMC has eight permanent members, and four rotating members, each having one vote.

Seven of the permanent members are the chairman and vice chairman of the Fed and five board members, the seven comprising what is known as the Board of Governors, also known as the "Board." Each member is appointed to the Board by our president for fourteen years, or for a lesser term if it is not an initial appointment.

For example, one person can receive an initial appointment to the Board for fourteen years, leave after five years, and be replaced by another person for the remaining nine years of the initial fourteen-year term. If the second person subsequently leaves after five years, a third person is appointed for the remaining four years of the initial fourteen-year period. This continues until the initial fourteen-year appointment period is totally used up, and it starts again with another person being appointed for a fourteen-year term.

These fourteen-year terms are staggered so that one expires every two years. So given the fact that a Board member seldom remains for the full fourteen-year term, and that in any event, one fourteen-year term expires every two years, a President has ample opportunity to influence a Board with his appointments.

Another provision is that no two Board members can come from the same Federal Reserve Bank district.

But this is more cosmetic than a requirement. In 1975 during President Nixon's Administration, the Board already had a member representing the Seventh Federal Reserve District (Chicago). Another person from the same district, Charles Partee, was about to be appointed by President Nixon to the Board. But since Partee had also lived for a short period of time in another Fed district, he was appointed to the Board representing Virginia, (the Fifth Fed District), rather than the Seventh District.

Within this fourteen-year-term structure, the president appoints a Fed chairman and vice chairman to serve for 4 years, thus enabling each new president to appoint his chairman and vice chairman. Theoretically, both a chairman and a vice chairman—if replaced by a president—could remain on the Board as members if there were time remaining on the fourteen-year term into which they were slotted, and if there were two other positions open on the Board. For practical purposes, however, this is not the case, although the first Fed chairman, Marriner Eccles, did remain on the Board after Thomas McCabe was appointed by President Truman to replace him in 1948.

The eighth permanent member of the FOMC is the president of the Federal Reserve Bank of New York, who by position is the vice chairman of the FOMC (not to be confused with the vice chairman of the Fed).

The four rotating member positions are shared by the other eleven Federal Reserve Bank presidents. Four of these presidents get to vote on the FOMC for one year, and are then replaced by four others for a year, etc. Thus, each of the eleven

Federal Reserve Banks get an equal amount of time for their president to sit on the FOMC as a voting member.

Usually all of the Federal Reserve Bank presidents attend and participate in all FOMC meetings, but there are always seven of these who are not eligible to vote.

Final-decision-making authority for the other 83 percent of things the Fed does rests solely with the Board of Governors. Each of the seven members has one vote on all matters.

Although each of the twelve Federal Reserve Banks has a board of directors, any important decisions that it makes, including those that have nationwide impact, must be forwarded to the Board of Governors in Washington for final approval. Thus, the governance authority of a Fed Bank Board is considerably more limited than that of any other board of directors in the private sector. Moreover, any decision it makes affecting only its Federal Reserve Bank territory (also known as its Fed District) must be consistent with the Board of Governors' policy on the matter. For example, when the board of directors of a Federal Reserve Bank desires to construct a new Bank building, it requires multiple Board approvals in Washington, from start to finish, as you will see. If it votes to change the discount rate in its Fed District, that decision must be approved by the Board in Washington.

In addition, the top two officers for each Federal Reserve Bank, the president and first vice president, must be approved by the Board of Governors in Washington before they can assume office. The appointment of other bank executives is delegated to the Bank's board.

The Federal Reserve Banks issue stock, which is purchased by member commercial banks. But unlike stock of a firm in the private sector whose earnings are either retained or paid out to stockholders, the billions of dollars of earnings of the Reserve Banks are paid into the general fund of the U.S. Treasury. A nominal dividend is paid by the Reserve Banks to member commercial banks on their stock.

Because Reserve Banks have boards of directors and issue stock, the Fed is often referred to as a "pseudo-governmental" organization. It has characteristics found in firms in the private sector, but operates much differently.

The Federal Reserve branches all have boards of directors as well, and these are subservient in decision-making authority to that of the board of directors of the Federal Reserve Banks, under which they operate. So the top two positions on the power scale in the Fed belong to the chairman, at the top, and the six other members of the Board of Governors who are second on the ladder. In third position is the Board's staff, particularly the senior advisors. They are in daily contact with the chairman and Board members, advise them on all relevant matters, and thus greatly influence their decisions.

Therefore, since each of the seven members of the Board of Governors has a vote, both on FOMC and all other matters, the power in the Fed clearly resides with the seven Board members. And of those seven, clearly it is the Fed chairman, who, by far, is the most powerful. And some Fed chairmen are more powerful than others. Intimidation, and other factors, come into play.

Let's now move behind the closed doors of the Fed.

3

Headquarters

The group of bankers had a pleasant flight into Washington's Reagan National Airport, from Cleveland—if you can call "pleasant" that last right turn over the Potomac just as you are about to land to the south. It was a typically beautiful fall day in the nation's capital. Washington has, perhaps, the best fall weather on the planet.

The bankers were on their way to the Fed's headquarters to meet with a relatively new Board member, Jack Sheehan, who was from the Sixth Fed District, which is served by the Federal Reserve Bank of Cleveland. Since most of the bankers had not previously been to Washington, Jack had arranged the full show for them, including a briefing and a tour of the Board's facilities.

After a short car ride along the Potomac, over the Memorial Bridge and past the Lincoln Memorial, they arrived at twenty-first Street and Constitution Avenue, and could see, just to the south. the Washington Monument, to the north, the signs reading "Board of Governors of the Federal Reserve System." They made a left turn and drove to the public entrance to the Board building, which is on C Street at the back of the building. After being screened by the security guards, they entered the building, and after a short greeting by Jack, started their tour and briefing.

Facilities and Atmosphere

The Fed's headquarters consists of two buildings: the Board building, which faces Constitution Avenue to the south; and the Martin Building, which is directly behind the Board building to the north, across C Street. The former was constructed in 1913, and the latter in the early 1970s. The Board also owns a building on New York Avenue in Washington, D.C. that was purchased in the 1990s and is partially leased. It houses the Fed's inspector general, among others.

The Board building was officially named after Marriner Eccles, the first Fed chairman, although all in the Fed refer to it as the "Board building" and not the "Eccles building."

The Martin Building was named after William McChesney Martin, the third Fed chairman, highly regarded, and credited with making the statement, "We take the punch bowl away just as the party gets going," in referring to the Fed's tightening actions when interest rates are driven up in order to combat inflation. It is known as the "Martin Building" inside the Fed.

Both buildings are white, the facade of the Board building being made of white Georgia marble and that of the Martin building also of white marble. From the sky, the Board building looks like a capital *H* lying on its side, whereas the Martin Building is rectangular. The buildings are not imposing by Washington standards. Perhaps the most prominent architecture is the wide front portico and front steps of the Board building facing Constitution Avenue. An underground tunnel below C Street connects the buildings.

The impressions that are conveyed to all entering Fed headquarters, and particularly the Board building, are conservatism, dignity, sedateness, and professionalism. The halls have marble floors, are tall, spacious, and quiet—except just prior to and after Board meetings. The offices are carpeted, tastefully furnished, and illuminated by table, desk, and floor lamps—thus providing a soft light and genteel atmosphere. Board staff and visitors alike approach these offices with deference, especially that of the chairman. Unless you are a Fed employee and accustomed to the surroundings, these accentuate—to all who visit—the mysterious aura of the Board of Governors, the technical and complex economic and operational matters to which they attend, and which the vast majority of the public does not understand.

Largest Conference Table in Washington

You enter the Board building at its rear on the north side, at street level, and proceed up a short marble stairway to the main floor, past the elevators and some offices, and arrive at the main corridor. The high ceilings and marble floors draw your attention and you think, "They don't construct buildings like this anymore."

Directly in front of you are two large doors opening into the Boardroom, where all Board and FOMC meetings are held. The room is large, has high ceilings and big chandeliers, and floor-to-ceiling windows looking southward on Constitution Avenue. Contained within the room is the largest conference table in Washington, which, from one end to the other, is about 50 feet long and 10 feet wide, and occupies about half of the room. There is a large fireplace on the west wall, and a private entrance door leading to and from the chairman's office. Opposite on the east wall is the door leading to the anteroom, used as a staging point by staff for presentations at Board and FOMC meetings, and by the press attending Board meetings.

The boardroom can be quite intimidating, especially when it is filled to capacity. It is easy for the inexperienced to be overwhelmed by the scene. Picture, if you will, the huge table with fifty to sixty chairs around it, all fully occupied by the Board members and staff. All of the approximately 100 chairs that are along the four walls of the room are also occupied. Many people are standing because all available seats are taken. TV cameras are on. Newspaper reporters are taking notes. Everyone in the room is focused on your every word as you present

17

your position on the matter under consideration by the Board. Any and all questions by the Board members are fair game.

I have seen many a budding staff career ruined by a bad performance in that room.

Some staff members attempt to deal with this anxiety by thinking, "I know more about these issues than anyone in the room, so relax."

Well, to begin with, you don't go to that table unless your preparation allows you to think that. And above all, you don't fake it. If you don't know the answer, you state so, and tell the Board that you will research the matter and get back to them.

But even then, the best preparation doesn't always work.

I recall presenting a matter to the Board, and Arthur Burns, who was then chairman, said, as I finished, "Mr. Kudlinski, you are just like the Soviet economists," and then paused, staring at me and awaiting my reply.

I didn't know what he was talking about, and started looking around the room for help. I turned to the two Board members, Jack Sheehan and Jeff Buecher, who worked closely with me on this matter, and both suddenly found the view out of the room's large windows irresistible. I could not get their attention, because they wouldn't give it to me.

Ditto, when I looked at Ron Burke, a division director, who also worked on this matter. He found something in the memorandum we prepared for the Board so interesting that he couldn't and wouldn't take his eyes off it—despite my nudging him as he was sitting to my right.

All the while, all eyes in the room were upon me—except for those of my three potential but unwilling rescuers—to see how I was going to get out of this.

Finally, after deafening silence, it occurred to me, after some prompting by Burns, that I had not taken into account the time value of money. (For example, receiving $1,000 five years from now has less value than receiving it today, and should be discounted to determine its present value. Soviet economists did not include the time value of money in their analyses.) Needless to say, I never again appeared in that room on any matter without being prepared if dollars were involved.

Every little slip can be embarrassing. I once responded to a Board member's question at that table by stating, "Governor, it only costs $30,000." Burns looked at me and said, "Mr. Kudlinski, $30,000 may not be a lot of money to you, but it is to me."

If you are part of the Fed, and Burns used to refer to it as being "part of the Fed family," you address a Board member as "Governor," and you address the Fed chairman as "mister chairman." Commercial bankers, businessmen, academicians, and other visitors to the Fed's headquarters do likewise. Its part of the tradition, as well as proper protocol, particularly during Board meetings.

Calendar

Board meetings are scheduled for Monday, Wednesday, and Friday of each week, with a 10 A.M. start time. Additional meetings also can be scheduled. When meetings are lengthy, a lunch break is taken, and the meetings resume about 2 P.M. In rare instances, they will continue on to the next day.

Preparation for a Board meeting is lengthy and detailed. The secretary to the Board (an official, and not an administrative position) has primary responsibility and consults with the chairman, Board members, and the officers of the Board in planning each meeting. (Officers of the Board are the staff members, who hold the positions of directors of divisions, associate directors, and assistant directors.)

Tentative agendas are planned for each Board meeting, days and weeks in advance, depending upon agenda content. Over time, the agenda is finalized. Each agenda has an action-item list, and a consent item list. The latter items are considered at the outset of a Board meeting and approved, en masse. Most consent lists are approved unanimously. Individual items on the consent list are occasionally "pulled" and deferred for further work, particularly if there are questions.

Items on the action list are considered separately at the Board meeting, and the chairman takes the vote of the Board members on each action item after all information is presented to the Board by staff.

The Board's secretary prepares the minutes for each meeting, which includes the votes, by name, of the Board members on each action item.

(The Board officially refers to the action list as the "action calendar," and the consent list as the "consent calendar.")

What kind of items end up on the Board's action list? The names of the eight staff divisions give you a good idea of the type of items the Board considers.

For example, the Division of Reserve Bank Operations and Payments Systems (which was known as the Division of Federal Reserve Bank Operations and Budgets when I was its director) will schedule matters concerned primarily with the operations, examinations, and budgets of the Fed Banks, branches, and offices; the regulations concerning banking operations nationwide; and payment system matters.

The Division of Research and Statistics will schedule items concerned primarily with economic issues in banking, and will address the economic issues in all matters considered by the Board.

The Division of Banking Supervision and Regulation will schedule matters concerned with the regulation and supervision of commercial banks nationwide, such as bank requests for expansion of permissible activities; competition in banking, including mergers and acquisitions; and commercial bank examinations.

The Division of Consumer and Community Affairs will schedule items concerned primarily with the impact of banking on consumers, such as limiting consumer liability in credit card use to $50 in the event of a stolen credit card. In essence, the division protects the consumer in banking and regulatory matters.

The Legal Division addresses legal matters in all items under consideration by the Board.

The Division of International Finance schedules items concerned with international banking.

The Division of Information Technology provides computer support to the Board and its staff divisions.

The Division of Monetary Affairs provides staff support to the Board and the FOMC on monetary-policy matters.

There is also an Office of Board Members, plus an Office of the Staff Director for Management, and a Management Division, and these groups assist the Board in administering to the Headquarters personnel and physical resources.

The amount of paperwork created for each Board meeting is enormous. For each action and consent item on an agenda, one or more memoranda may be prepared by each of the eight staff Divisions. So a Board member may have a stack of papers 6–12 inches high to read and digest before every meeting. I am told that our congressional legislators also have mountainous stacks of papers to consume. The difference is that Board members actually read their material.

Andrew Brimmer, a Board member in the 1970s, standardized the content of staff memoranda that go to the Board members to assist them in assimilating the information rapidly. It's still in use today. Each memorandum contains the following:

Header Information
    From:
    To:
    Subject:
    References:
    Action Requested:
    Recommendation:

Discussion Sections
    Issues:
    Background:
    Discussion:
    Conclusions and Recommendations:

The Header Information section contains one- or two-sentence items and enables a Board member to quickly review content to determine if additional reading is required—in which case, the discussion sections will provide details.

Each of the memoranda is very carefully and professionally prepared and as tightly written as possible, and becomes part of the official record of the Board.

In order to be successful at the Board as a member of staff, you have to be an outstanding communicator, both verbally and in writing. And you must be able to think and analyze rapidly on your feet—on the fly, so to speak. Staff members who are successful and develop a good reputation eventually move into the financial industry, some at a substantial increase in pay.

Presidential Appointees and Conflict

How does one become a Board member?

The necessary political connections that will result in your name being considered by the White House for the position are the first step in the process. Beyond that, it's a matter of bettering the competition for the position, which involves political as well as nonpolitical considerations. The White House will consult with the Fed chairman in this process, and some chairmen have had more influence than others.

Board members come from all backgrounds, including academic, legal, industrial, business management, manufacturing, economic, banking, and from within the Fed, both from Board staff and from Federal Reserve Banks.

All of the Board members that I have worked with were successful in their respective career fields before joining the Board. Insofar as I could determine, this is true of those Board members who were there before me, as well as those afterward. The presidential appointment process ensures that high-quality and successful career individuals are selected as Board members.

The Board member position is an honor to the recipient. After all, there are only seven of these in the entire country, including the chairman's.

Indeed, fame and notoriety accompany the Fed chairman's position. Once in this position, you are constantly quoted in the print and TV media.

The other Board members, however, including the vice chairman of the Fed, do not enjoy such international and national prominence. They are known in banking circles, and somewhat in the financial industry, but, for the most part, work in relative obscurity behind the closed doors of the Fed. Because of the vote on all Board matters that they are entitled to, once they are confirmed by the Senate and actually seated on the Board, the position is one of the most powerful available in the public sector in this nation.

Some Board members take to the Federal Reserve System like a fish to water. They enjoy it, are successful, and leave their mark. Others, for various reasons, are less successful—or even unsuccessful.

For example, a Board member that I worked with believed that he was promised the vice chairman position—he felt slighted when it didn't happen, and eventually lost interest and resigned. Some are given responsibilities on the Board that are inconsistent with their background and experience and they spend most of their time trying to catch up. And some leave the Board for economic reasons—such as, to regain control of their financial assets. These had had to be placed in a blind trust before one's having been seated on the Board.

Overall, however, most Board members are successful during their time at the Fed. The most successful of all was former vice chairman George Mitchell. I will say a lot more about him and his accomplishments both as a Board member and as vice chairman, during his sixteen years at Headquarters, later in this book. He was able to do what no other Board member could do—not those before him, and not those after him. And I might add, he was the only Board member I ever heard address Burns as "Arthur" rather than as "Mr. chairman." As a matter of fact, he was the only person ever heard to do that. All others—bankers, congressmen, Fed people, etc.—did not. George Mitchell and Burns had a very good working relationship, Burns relied heavily on Mitchell, and Mitchell produced.

People who stood out above the pack as Board members, when I was there, included Jack Sheehan, an industrialist; Jeff Buecher, an attorney from commercial banking, Andrew Brimmer, an economist; Steve Gardner, a commercial banker; Henry Wallick, an academician and economist, Phil Jackson, a mortgage banker, David Lilly, an industrialist, Fred Schultz, a commercial banker, and Phil Coldwell, Bob Holland, Chuck Partee, and Lyle Gramley, former Federal Reserve employees.

Five of the outstanding Board members were from inside the Fed. Mitchell came from the Federal Reserve Bank of Chicago; Holland's background was from the Federal Reserve Bank of Chicago and the Board staff; Coldwell was the president of the Federal Reserve Bank of Dallas when he took a large cut in pay to join the Board; and Chuck Partee and Lyle Gramley were both directors of the Division of Research and Statistics at the Board. (Gramley left the Board to serve on the Council of Economic Advisers in the then President Carter's Administration, and then returned as a Board member.)

When you have the benefit of experience in the Fed, and you have learned how to get things done in the Fed, it then surfaces when you become a Board member. These five had that advantage and were very successful in the position.

Conflicts do arise, from time to time, between the Fed chairman, Board members, and staff, but these are not a common occurrence.

Conflicts between the chairman and Board members usually involve a Board members making public statements about an issue in advance of the full Board's establishing its position and voting on the matter. That is considered a large faux pas in the Fed. You never get in front of the Board on anything if you wish to survive in the Fed.

The most extreme of this type of situation occurred during Burns's tenure. In the mid-1970s, a board member, just prior to resigning, made a speech to a New York group in which he divulged information prior to the full Board's taking action on the matter. It was his last speech as a Board member and he wanted to make a newsworthy, substantive presentation. He was soon confronted by Burns.

A short time afterward after leaving the Board, he attended a Fed-sponsored social gathering. I attended also and was standing and talking to the former Board member when he said, "Move about three steps to your right, and he "hunched" down. I looked him in the eye, then turned around and saw Burns enter the room—he was hiding from Burns, and using me as a shield.

I have seen Board members get upset with their colleagues, particularly when one Board member invades another's "turf." They do not look kindly upon a colleague who usurps their responsibilities. One Board member, for example, in anger, offered his colleague his "proxy" vote on all matters for which they were jointly responsible—because he was left out of the decision process on an issue with which the two were involved.

There are conflicts that occur between Board members and staff, but these lie beneath the surface and fester, rather than resulting in any confrontation. Typical of these are those instances when a Board member perceives to be, or is actually, "slighted" by staff. Some Board members can take the high road and forgive and forget. Others are like elephants, they never forget.

For example, a situation occurred between a Board member and a senior staff person who had arranged an early-morning meeting. The Board member showed up, but the staff person forgot about the arrangement and didn't show up. The Board member later brought the matter to the staff person's attention and stated, "I guess you had an emergency situation and, therefore, couldn't make the meeting." Rather than inventing some excuse, the staff person apologized and stated he just forgot about it. The Board member turned away in anger, and from that day forward, he never forgot the "slight"—and went out of his way to make things difficult for the staff person.

There are also conflicts that occur among staff members at the Board. Mine were all with the Division of Research and Statistics.

The Board's research staff in those days (the middle to late 1970s) had a penchant for inferring possible world-altering consequences from the transition to EFT (electronic funds transfer) in our nation's payments mechanism. This became an in-house joke among some of us—and it also could be quite annoying and frustrating, particularly when you were attempting to get something done (or not done). At one meeting we had with Mitchell, during which we were reviewing the latest research staff memorandum to the Board on EFT developments, he said, "What do these guys think, people are going to stop screwing because we have EFT?" Jim Brundy, Al Raiken, and I got a big laugh out of that one.

Brundy is an interesting guy. He has an undergraduate degree from Harvard, and a Ph.D. in economics from Cal Tech. He had attended Yale Law School for one year, gotten bored, returned to the Board, and completed his law degree at Georgetown while working full-time as part of the Board's research staff. After I left the Board, I later hired him away from the Bank of America to run some financial institutions.

Raiken is an attorney, and a very good one. Mitchell and I relied on his advice extensively. He later left the Board and enjoyed a successful career in the private sector.

On another occasion, the Board was in the process of publishing Subpart B of Regulation J for public comment—this subpart set forth the legal framework for the Fed's handling of electronic payments. (The Board always publishes proposed banking regulations for comment prior to implementation—sometimes on multiple occasions, depending upon the alterations required in the regulation from comments received.) Concurrently, a major revision was being considered internally within the Fed for the pricing of its services.

Up until that time, Fed services had been given to member commercial banks of the Federal Reserve System and only members had direct access to such services. All other financial institutions, including nonmember commercial banks, savings and loans associations, mutual savings banks, and credit unions, had to access Fed services through a member bank. Since it was essential, in the conduct of business, for a financial institution to have access to Fed services, this arrangement gave member banks a monopoly, and allowed them to set and extract the "toll" (fee) that all other financial institutions would have to pay to them to use such essential services.

Former vice chairman Mitchell was the catalyst in bringing this matter to the Board's attention, and in instigating revisions that provided a level playing field to all financial institutions and their access to Fed services. One of the key ingredients was the principle of pricing for Fed services that previously had been given away free to only member banks as a quid pro quo for the "reserves" that they had to maintain with the Fed. Subsequent chapters deal with how this was done. Here let's concentrate on the pricing for services issue. (Eventually, the Monetary Control Act of 1980 legislatively made it mandatory for the Fed to price for its services.)

The research staff strongly recommended to the Board that it publish prices for Fed services in conjunction with Subpart B of Regulation J, and request public comment on both. My division, as well as the operating unit management of the Reserve Banks, took a strong position against doing so. The matter was resolved at a Saturday morning meeting with the then chairman Burns in his office.

The research staffers presented their arguments for publishing the prices for comment, and I presented the arguments against doing so.

After considerable discussion of the matter, Burns turned to me and said, "Mr. Kudlinski, do you wish to withhold the actual price and request comment only on the principle that we will price for services because you believe the prices suggested by research can be lowered, or increased, depending upon the comments we get?"

I immediately saw where he was headed, and answered, "Either one, Mr. chairman."

He looked at the assembled group and said, "I prefer Mr. Kudlinski's approach."

John Mingo, an officer on the Board's research staff who had headed their efforts on this, looked like he had gotten to the fourth quarter of the game and lost in the last minute.

The research staff was not used to losing many "economic"-type arguments before the Fed chairman.

Afterward, Al Raiken mentioned to me, as we were leaving Burns's office, "You and the chairman hit it off."

Conflicts such as these were the rule, rather than the exception, between operating management and research people in the Fed. Reputations were on the line, and no one wanted to lose the intellectual arguments and be embarrassed in front of their colleagues, the Board, and the chairman.

Fireplaces and Art

On either side of the boardroom are the Board members' offices, the chairman having the only private entry and exit to the room.

All of the Board members' offices are essentially alike. All are comfortably spacious, have working fireplaces; floor-to-ceiling windows facing Constitution Avenue; sufficient space for furniture, including a large desk and sofas, chairs, and tables; and private bathrooms. All have wood parquet flooring and attractive area rugs. A car and a driver are made available to all Board members that they may use when acting in an official capacity. (Federal Reserve Bank presidents have similar office space and car and driver services.)

Outside each Board member's office is a smaller office for a secretary. Some have used multiple secretaries.

Occasionally, some Board members do special things with

their offices. Jack Sheehan purchased his own office furniture and did not use any out of Fed storage, and, of course, took it with him when he left. George Mitchell displayed some of the art he collected over the years while vacationing in Taos, New Mexico, an art colony.

Speaking of art, a little-known fact is that there is a display of art throughout the Board and Martin buildings—some of which is quite valuable. For example, I admired a Renoir work in the Special Library of the Board building whenever I went there for a meeting. The Board permits owners of art to house and display their art at Fed Headquarters in climate controlled and secured space. Insurance is provided by the Board for such art on display. There is an art consultant on the Board's staff who manages the program on a full-time basis. If you are holding a valuable piece of art for appreciation, that is not a bad place to house it.

Best in the Capital

The first thing you are impressed with when you begin working at the Board is the high quality and professional staff members that are there. Virtually every Board member makes this comment after being there for a short time. So do people from other government organizations, including congressional staff members after having had the opportunity to work and interface with them.

In the Research and Statistics, and Legal Divisions, the Board is successful in attracting the top graduates in economics and law from the top-rated schools in the nation. The quality of the staff in these two Divisions surpasses that found in the other divisions—although there are some very smart people in the other divisions. The problem is that the quality of people in the other divisions is not as consistently outstanding as they are throughout all pay grades in those two divisions.

Two of the outstanding ones while I was there were Dave Humphrey and Ed Ettin, both economists. Dave subsequently left the Board to head up the research area in a Reserve Bank, and then moved to the private sector. Ed remained with the Board, and for 40 years was instrumental in formulating Board policy in the economic area.

The Board has the same pay scale as the rest of the Federal government. The Board's pay grades are known as "FR," as contrasted with "GS" ratings, through pay grade 18, and continue on to what is known as "senior executive service" pay levels.

What does this all mean? The chairman of the Fed's pay is equal to that of a U.S. senator; Board members' pay equals that of a congressman; and senior staff members can achieve a pay level equal to that of a congressman.

But the Board also pays bonuses (now known as merit increases) to its senior staff people, which means that the highest paid Board staff members make more than the chairman and Board members, on the order of $180,000–200,000 per year. This is less than what the highest-paid officers earn who work in the Federal Reserve Banks, but not too much less.

In 2005, the top-paid employees in the Fed were the presidents of the Federal Reserve Banks of Boston, Atlanta, Chicago, and Minneapolis, each making $355,600. The Cleveland Fed had the lowest-paid president at $249,000. All of the other salaried employees at Fed Banks earn a lesser amount than the president, including the top-paid officers.

If you are good at what you do and develop a reputation, you can use the Fed as a stepping stone to more attractive positions outside the Fed and substantial pay increases, in many cases. I have seen Fed staff members increase their pay by as much as 1,000 percent when moving into the private sector.

Who Does the Work?

There is a very unusual nuance at the Board in the way things get done, and who ends up doing the majority of the meaningful staff work.

I was once asked a question by Rolf Engler while we were in an elevator with two Board members on our way up to the Fed's dining facilities in the Martin Building. Rolf was visiting the Board from the Bundesbank, Germany's central bank. His question was, "How many people work here?" I answered, "About 20 percent." He laughed.

I said that because the same 20 percent of Board staff appear at all Board meetings and handle all relevant matters. What do the other 80 percent do? Make-work type projects, and they support the 20 percent that do all the work.

The Board is a very benevolent employer. You have to do something really bad to be fired. I can remember only one person being fired during the entire time I was there, and that occurred in the mid-1970s when Burns was chairman. That individual passed some information to a reporter that was "in-house"-eyes-only-type material on FOMC matters. The information appeared in the morning paper, the *Wall Street Journal*. By noon of that same day, the employee's desk was cleared out and he was gone.

What usually happened if you were not successful as a staff member at the Board was the following: (1) you were given office space; (2) projects to do; and (3) you got your in-grade step increase in pay every two years. Many stayed on and survived while some took the hint and looked elsewhere.

I would always tell someone in that position in my division that I thought he or she should begin to look elsewhere, and the person usually did, and successfully made the move to the private sector.

Watergate and the Martin Building

The Martin Building housed all of the Board's staff—with the exception of the Divisions of Research and Statistics and Legal, which were in the Board building.

Before the Martin Building was constructed, a large portion of the Board staff that ultimately occupied the building was housed in the Watergate Office Building. Yes, the same building in which the burglary took place that ultimately caused President Nixon's resignation. My office was located two floors directly above the Democratic Headquarters office space.

Many may not recall, but the Fed had a direct hand in apprehending the Watergate burglars.

Because Fed offices in the Watergate building were being broken into and equipment and supplies were stolen, Fed security guards were hired to secure the area.

On the night in question, one of those Fed security guards, while making his rounds, noticed that the lock on the secure door leading from the building to the parking garage was taped open so that the lock wouldn't function. You could walk from the garage into the building through the door that was ordinarily locked after working hours. He removed the tape, which locked the door, and proceeded on his rounds. When he again found the door taped open on his next round, he alerted the authorities and the rest is history.

The size of an office in the Martin Building is dependent on your position. Division directors have the largest offices, about the size of Board members, and private bathrooms. The size of the offices decreases as you proceed down the pay scale. Most of the building consists of small, two-person offices in which professional staff members are located.

Also included in the Martin Building are the cafeteria, the officers' dining room, and private dining rooms, the latter being used by Board members and senior staff for breakfast and luncheon meetings. There is also a room in the Martin Building that can accommodate large parties for meetings as well as for breakfasts and luncheons.

All food service is subsidized—so that prices are attractive to all employees. The quality of the food is surprisingly good.

Federal Reserve Banks and branches have food facilities and services similar to that of the Board.

It is not unusual for the chairman of the Fed and the Board members to host breakfast and luncheon meetings with dignitaries from Congress, presidential administrations, and the domestic and international banking and business sectors. I have attended many of these, and surprisingly, some turn out to be productive meetings.

There is one meeting, however, that stands out in my memory, not for its productive value, but rather, as an incident you don't forget. I have to present some background information before I get into it.

Fed representatives meet periodically with those from the Bank for International Settlements (BIS), located in Basel, Switzerland. Think of the BIS as a bank for "central banks," as the Fed is a bank for "commercial banks" and other financial depositories.

The Fed meets periodically with central bank representatives from the developed countries, including Germany, Italy, France, England, Canada, Japan, and Belgium, to discuss and exchange banking information. Of course, BIS representatives also participate.

The incident I recall here happened when we met at the Fed's headquarters in the late 1970s, in the large meeting room in the Martin Building, to discuss and exchange information on payment-mechanism developments in each of our countries.

The modus operandi of this particular BIS group was for each country to take a turn at hosting a meeting for all participants, and it was now the Fed's turn. Alcohol is not normally served in the Board's dining facilities, but this was a special occasion. Europeans make it a practice of having wine with their meals, so the Fed served wine at the luncheon.

After lunch, I went to the men's room and ran into Kevin Kearney, a staff member of the BIS who worked directly for Dr. Gunther Schleiminger, who was then the assistant general manager of the BIS and the number-two man in the organization.

Schleiminger had an unusual past. He was a communications technician on a U-boat during World War II. He was a thin man, ate sparingly, and one of the best hosts I have ever had the pleasure of meeting.

33

Kevin is an American from the New England area who joined the employ of the BIS after having held various positions in computer-related fields. He speaks multiple languages, including German, French, Italian, and Spanish—which is almost mandatory if you work for the BIS. He had an interesting home in Basel that he rented from a family that has had ownership of the property for over 200 years. He retired to a chalet that he built in the Swiss Alps.

Kevin is a good friend of mine. I had been to his home in Basel many times. Kevin is the only person I have met who could really claim to be a wine connoisseur. He knows wines and has over 1,500 bottles in his cellar.

In any event, I asked Kevin what he thought about the wine the Fed had served with lunch. It was Rothschild Mouton Cadet, both the red and the white, a French wine. I said that I thought it was very good, and that the Board went out of its way to serve a quality wine.

Kevin said, "You know Jim, I'm very familiar with that wine. Schleiminger gave me three bottles for Christmas. It's an average to mediocre wine, costing about eight fifty to nine dollars per bottle. I know, because I checked the price."

Just then the commode right in front of us flushed and we heard the "whoosh." The stall door was thrown open, hit the wall, and out emerged Schleiminger. He proceeded directly to a sink to wash his hands—not looking at or saying anything to either of us.

I watched Kevin the whole time, and his eyes were the size of quarters, and I swear, red coloring was proceeding up his neck, through his cheeks, and through his forehead—just like a thermometer.

After drying his hands, Schleiminger exited the men's room. I looked back at Kevin as I was about to leave. His mouth was agape, he was staring vacantly at the door, and he murmured, "Oh, shit . . ."

The visiting group of bankers from Cleveland completed their tour and briefing at the Fed's headquarters. Afterward, they joined Jack Sheehan for lunch in one of the private dining rooms in the Martin Building.

Jack is an interesting guy. He came to the Board from a CEO position with a subsidiary of Corning Glass, located in Ohio. He was a classmate of Ross Perot's at the Naval Academy, with whom he remained in touch, and had an MBA from the Harvard Business School.

Ross Perot

When I decided to leave the Fed and move to the private sector, Jack Sheehan suggested that I prepare a business plan on the provision of electronic payment services to financial institutions—and that he would send it to Ross Perot.

Electronic payment services had not yet developed in the nation. There was much discussion going on as to how these might develop and who the alternative providers of such services might be. The large banks were making claims to the turf, and the small and medium-sized banks, S&Ls, mutual savings banks, and credit unions were uncomfortable in having a competitor control such facilities and the price of access thereto.

As a result, President Carter appointed the Commission on Electronic Funds Transfer Systems to study the area and to make recommendations to Congress on the matter. The report of the commission ultimately was transformed into legislation governing the development of electronic funds-transfer systems (EFTS) in this country.

George Mitchell was one of the members of this Presidential Commission, the Federal Reserve System representative, and the most influential on the commission. He had retired from the Fed and was retained by the Board as a consultant for this purpose.

I worked closely with Mitchell on these matters—and this, as well as being at the Board and at the locus of developments and information interchange on EFTS matters, allowed me to be in a unique position to assess what could be done realistically and by whom as far as the development of EFTS was concerned in this country.

EDS (Electronic Data Services), a Texas corporation owned and controlled by Ross Perot at the time, was in a unique position to become the principal provider of EFTS services to financial institutions and their customers. They were already providing computer services to a myriad of financial institutions. And it would be a natural extension to include the provision of EFTS services in their product mix. Moreover, not being a financial institution, they would not be considered a "competitor" and would be much better accepted by the small and medium-sized institutions as a provider of such services than would a large bank.

I developed the business plan and gave it to Sheehan. About a week later, I received a call from Ross Perot. He read the plan, which Sheehan sent to him, said he was interested, and suggested I come down to Dallas to meet with him and his staff—which I did on more than one occasion.

Perot's office was decorated in a western motif, including more than one Remington sculpture and paintings. But the focus of his office decorations was a group of portraits of his wife and children hanging on the wall. Since Jack Sheehan's Board office also contained portraits of his wife and children, I could not help wondering who came up with the idea first, Ross or Jack.

I had made a few trips to Dallas, time was moving on, and I had been offered a job outside the Fed, which appealed to me.

I called Perot and told him that I had to have his decision on whether or not he was going to pursue the business plan—because I was ready to leave the Fed. He told me, "If you have to have my decision today, I'm going to have to say no. I am tied up with a three-hundred- fifty-million-dollar law suit, which is taking my total attention."

(EDS had acquired a brokerage firm in Manhattan that resulted in major legal and other problems, which ultimately were dealt with successfully.)

I left the Fed, and I (and Perot) abandoned the business

plan—which, in hindsight, was a shortsighted thing to do. If we had successfully accomplished what I was proposing, EDS would have had a fee from most of the cash dispensing, ATM, and point-of-sale transactions in this nation—and I, of course, would have participated. I regret the decision.

These Guys Are Good

Every Board member, after being nominated by the president for a position on the Board of Governors of the Federal Reserve System, must go through an "acceptance hearing" before the Senate Banking Committee. The nominees prepared for this by Board staff.

During Jack Sheehan's acceptance hearing before the Senate Banking Committee, he was asked a number of questions by a senator. To some of these questions, Jack replied, "Just a minute," searched for and found the question in the briefing book had been prepared for him by the research staff at the Board, and read the answer.

After referring to the briefing book for the fifth time, the senator interrupted Jack and asked what he was doing. Jack then told him about the briefing book. The senator was amazed, and said, "I'll be darned. How did they know what questions I would ask even before I asked them."

I told you earlier about the quality of the research staff. These guys are good—like the PGA golfers in the TV commercial.

In any event, lunch was over and the visiting group of bankers from Cleveland were enjoying coffee and dessert.

One of the bankers, a friend of Jack's, said, "Jack, you have been here for just under two years, so you have had a good opportunity to see what goes on. What can you tell us about the Fed? What's it like?"

Jack paused for a minute and looked out the window on to the Fed's two tennis courts behind the Martin Building as he was contemplating his answer. He then said: " I want you to imagine a big mound of Jello, a pyramid, about four to five feet tall, right in the middle of this table. Imagine walking up to that mound and punching it as hard as you can. And then kicking it as hard as you can. And then hitting it with your shoulder as hard as you can. And then punching it and kicking it again. While you are doing this, it shakes, and it shimmies, and it waddles back and forth. Then you step back and do nothing but watch it. The shaking, shimmying, and waddling slow down, and eventually, stop. And when it does, that mound of Jello looks just like it did before you started . . ."

4

Decision Making in the Fed

Jack's description of how difficult it was to move the Fed in any direction while he was there in the 1970s is not exaggerated. This conservative and bureaucratic central bank had evolved over time into a national organization—with a widespread international impact—that carefully, thoroughly, and thoughtfully considered its every move. Its management and decision-making by consensus had been systematically structured over the years to permit the Fed to do just that.

How did we get something done in the Fed during Jack's time on the Board, and for that matter, until the early 1990s?

Let's first consider the apparatus for the things the Fed does that 83 percent of its annual expenditures are directed toward. Then we'll look more closely at the apparatus for the other 17 percent of what it does—monetary policy.

Three Organizational Structures

There are three organizational structures within the Fed that handle matters of nationwide impact, and they act interdependently with one another:

1. Committees of the Board of Governors;
2. the Conference of First Vice Presidents of the Federal Reserve Banks; and
3. the Conference of Presidents of the Federal Reserve Banks.

Board Committees

The Board's seven members are assigned to committees of the Board by the Fed chairman, with consultation and input from the Board members, including the vice chairman.

Each committee of the Board has a designated chairman, and one or more members. So it is possible for a Board member to be a chairman of one or more committees, and a member of others.

The action and consent items that are scheduled on the Board's calendar that have a nationwide impact usually appear on the agendas of committees of the Board before being scheduled on the Board's calendar. Thus, these items are reviewed and recommendations are made by the committees to the full Board.

The Board's staff works with the committees in this process, and also with the full Board when the items are considered at a Board meeting.

(The items that do not have a nationwide impact also appear on committees' agendas. For example, a Federal Reserve Bank may request approval of an item that only pertains to the bank, but which requires Board approval—such as renovating or constructing a Bank building.)

Some committees have delegated authority from the Board to act upon and make final decisions on certain items on behalf of the full Board. Of course such delegated items are not scheduled on the Board's calendar. The delegated authority to Committees is limited. Anything of nationwide scope and impact must be approved by the full Board.

So let's begin to build that "big mound of jello," that pyramid that Jack talked about.

At the top of the pyramid is the Board of Governors, who have final decision-making authority in the Fed; one level below are the committees of the Board; and one level below those are the staff divisions of the Board. This structure was in place at the headquarters when Jack was there, and it still is today.

As action and consent items for eventual placement on the

Board of Governors

Board Committees

Staff Divisions

Board's calendar proceed up this pyramid, these are analyzed and recommendations on each item are made by the staff, then by Board committees, and finally, the seven-member Board makes the final decision. Thus, there are three layers of review and approval required after items reach Fed Headquarters for full Board consideration.

Where did these items come from during Jack's tenure—and until the early 1990s?

Let's continue building this pyramid.

Conference of First Vice presidents

Each of the first vice presidents of the twelve Federal Reserve Banks is a member of the Conference of First Vice Presidents. Prior to the early 1990s, the conference studied, reviewed, and made recommendations to the Board of Governors on issues concerning Federal Reserve Bank operations that had a nationwide impact. The Board members often requested that the conference study certain matters, or alternately, there was consensus among the conference members that such matters be studied.

The conference, like the Board, was subdivided into committees that dealt with designated issues and areas of responsibility. A member of the conference could be a chairman of one or more committees, and a member of others.

Each committee, in turn, designated one or more subcommittees to study and analyze assigned issues. Subcommittee members usually were senior executives from Reserve Banks, appointed because of their knowledge, background, and capability in the area under study.

Each subcommittee, in turn, designated one or more task forces wherein the detailed analysis was done. Task force members usually were mid-to-low level Reserve Bank executives or managers who had expertise and hands-on experience in the operational areas under study. They were selected to serve on these task forces also because of their reputation as being able to produce.

Before we go further, let's complete the pyramid that we started earlier:

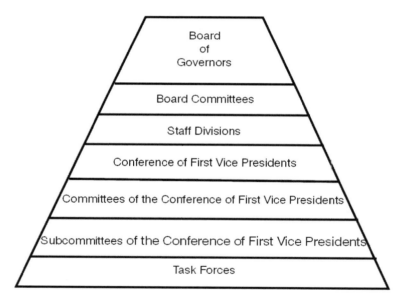

A task force did the detailed analysis and forwarded recommendations to the subcommittee, which in turn analyzed and reviewed the task force's work and forwarded recommendations to the committee, which in turn reviewed and analyzed the subcommittee's work and forwarded recommendations to the Conference; the Conference then reviewed and analyzed the Committee's work and forwarded recommendations to Fed Headquarters. This added four more layers of review and approval to the three described earlier at Fed Headquarters, for a total of seven.

Many committees of the Conference appointed multiple subcommittees to study an area thoroughly and many subcommittees appointed multiple task forces for the same reasons. As items worked their way up this pyramid, it is readily apparent that a consensus built with each step up.

This is because there were many Fed people involved from virtually all Federal Reserve Districts. By the time the Conference's final report on the matter was sent to Fed Headquarters, there was agreement among all Federal Reserve Districts on the course of action recommended.

The advantage to this method of management and decision-making by consensus was that errors were less likely, and that everyone was "going" in the same direction by the time you actually did something. And since the matter had been studied and analyzed "to death," as commercial bankers would say, you were confident in what you were going to do. Very rarely did the Fed ever make an error in decisions as a result of this "bottoms up" consensus-building management and decision-making system.

The major disadvantage to the system was the time and expense that it took to reach the consensus. Private-sector organizations would find it difficult to successfully replicate such a system. Moreover, they just couldn't afford it.

Normally, someone from the Board's staff was appointed to each task force and subcommittee, and occasionally even to a committee. The most knowledgeable staff member with expertise in the area under study was chosen. The reasons for such inclusion of a Board staff member are many—but the paramount reason was to ensure that the Board was kept abreast of developments and would not raise objections after all work was done. If alterations were necessary to accommodate the Board's concerns, these could be included early on.

Inside the Fed, people welcomed opportunities to serve on task forces, subcommittees, and Committees of the Conference. You could quickly become noticed with an outstanding performance—and gain a reputation that put you in demand for such service. Good things happened to you inside the Fed when this occurred.

Of course, the corollary was that bad performance could ruin your career.

Serving on these organizational entities was done in addition to your day-to-day responsibilities at the Fed. So you burned the "candle" at both ends. The people in the Fed who stood out for their work on these groups, particularly on the Fed's payments-mechanism matters, included Brown Rawlings, Atlanta; Howard Crumb, New York; Len Fernelius, Minneapolis; Jim Phelps, Atlanta; Tony Salvaggio, Dallas; Don Moriority, St. Louis; Dick Anstee, Chicago; Tom Hunt and Jim Mcintosh, Boston; Bruce Smith, Harry Schultz, and Dan Doyle, Chicago; Dale Cunningham, Richmond; Bill Hendricks, Cleveland; Jay Mast, Kansas City; and Tom Waage, New York.

The Board committees often requested that the Conference study and make recommendations on certain issues of nationwide importance. Some Board members knew how to do this better than others—such as how to push that "big pyramid of jello" to get it moving and to come to closure on areas under study more rapidly than ordinarily would be the case. Mitchell was a master at doing this, as I will note in later chapters.

Conference of Presidents

The structure for dealing with issues with nationwide impact in the Conference of Presidents was identical to that of the Conference of First Vice Presidents. The pyramids looked exactly alike and functioned in the same manner. The difference, however, was in the type of issues dealt with.

As indicated earlier, the Conference of First Vice Presidents dealt with operational matters, whereas that of the presidents focused on monetary policy, research and statistics, and supervision and regulation of member commercial banks.

$50 Million Mistake

Errors did occur at the Fed, but not when the "pyramid" was employed in studying and deciding on a course of action. Sometimes the "pyramid" was bypassed in the interest of expediency, or for other reasons.

I recall an interesting incident involving the Federal Reserve Bank of Philadelphia during Burns's tenure as Fed chairman. The Philadelphia Fed decided to create its own unique computer software for the clearing and settlement of checks that were deposited with it for collection by member commercial banks. (When you deposit a check with your bank, your bank conditionally credits your account, and then gives the check to the Fed and, in essence, says, "Go collect these funds for me from the bank on which this check is drawn, and put the funds into my account.")

The Philadelphia Fed implemented this software—not realizing it contained errors. As a result, cash letters were created that were out of balance.

A cash letter lists, among other things, all of the checks that a Fed office presents to a bank for payment, as well as the total amount that bank owes the Fed for those checks. For example, you write a check to your electric company to pay your bill. That check is deposited by your electric company in its bank, and its bank, in essence, gives that check to the Fed and says, "Go and collect the funds for me on this check from your bank."

By the time the Philadelphia Fed realized what was going on, the out-of-balance condition approached $50 million. The situation was so convoluted that it was not repairable, and the Philadelphia Fed had to write off the entire amount. They dis-

45

carded their unique software and implemented software that had proven to work in other Fed banks—which had been developed through the pyramid approach.

Afterward, the first vice president of the Philadelphia Fed, Mark Willes, came to our offices at Fed Headquarters and asked me if there was any way he could save his job. He also visited with others at Headquarters about the same matter.

Mark, as first vice president, was the chief operating officer of the Philadelphia Fed and, therefore, ultimately responsible for the loss—it had happened on his watch.

A few months later, I came into my office one morning and was met by some of my staff, including Brian Carey, who was an assistant director overseeing computer development at the Fed. He said to me, "Kudlinski, you know what's wrong with you? You just haven't fucked up bad enough." I looked at him questioningly and he stated, "Mark Willes was just appointed president of the Federal Reserve Bank of Minneapolis."

So there you have it. Mark's decision cost the Fed $50 million and they promote him to president. Remember, I said to you earlier that the Fed is a benevolent employer? I wasn't kidding.

In all fairness to Mark, he was a bright young fellow and probably went along with his staff when he should not have. Mark has a Ph.D. in economics and was a student of Burns's at Columbia. He did well as president of the Minneapolis Fed, and then had a successful career in the private sector as an executive with General Mills and Time Warner, after which I lost track of him.

Moreover, in my judgment, he was much better suited for the job of president of a Federal Reserve Bank than that of first vice president. The latter is an operating management type job, whereas the former requires an economic background such as Mark's. In this regard, we had an unwritten rule among some of us at Fed Headquarters: "Never hire an economist or an attorney to manage anything."

Today's Structure

Under Fed chairman Greenspan and continuing now under Bernanke, a substantial amount of control over the Fed's operations has been delegated to the Federal Reserve Banks, and a totally new structure for dealing with systemwide operations has evolved since the early 1990s.

A Financial Services Policy Committee has been established under the auspices of the Conference of Presidents, and this committee provides strategic direction and operational management of Fed services nationwide. The services that the Fed now provides are developed by seven Federal Reserve Banks, each specializing in a certain service area, as follows:

Atlanta—retail payments (such as check collection)
New York—wholesale payment products (such as wire transfers of funds)
San Francisco—cash products (currency and coin services)
St Louis—U.S. Treasury relations and support (the Fed provides banking services to the Treasury and other governmental organizations)
Chicago—customer relations and support offices
Boston—financial support offices
Richmond—business strategy offices

In addition, an Information Technical Oversight Committee has also been established under the Conference of Presidents to provide strategic direction and central computer and networking services to support Fed operations nationwide, including the seven "development centers" noted above. In conjunction with this committee, the Fed operates three mainframe computer centers in the New York area (East Rutherford, New Jersey), Dallas, and Richmond, which support Fed services nationwide.

This structure represents a dramatic change from the way in which Fed services were developed during Jack's time on the

Board—and until the early 1990s. The pyramid structure was employed exclusively in studying matters that had a systemwide impact. Parameters were established that provided guidelines for each Fed Bank in developing services for its local constituency. Thus, there were twelve Fed Banks designing and developing Fed services, each in accord with Board-approved systemwide parameters. And each Fed Bank operated its own computer mainframes.

Today's structure permanently "houses" responsibility for planning, developing, and implementing Fed services at seven Reserve Banks, each specializing in a certain area. What each designs and develops is then implemented nationwide at the twelve Reserve Banks, supported by the three-mainframe computer facilities.

This new structure evolved primarily because of advances in computer and networking technology—which provided the capability to support multiple Reserve Banks with one remote mainframe computer (or a few) controlling automated equipment used for Fed services locally. For example, each Fed office no longer required a computer to drive its check-processing sorters. These could instead be driven by a remote mainframe shared by all Fed offices.

And the Board's role in all of this has become one of "oversight," with much less action requiring full Board approval today than was the case during Jack's tenure at Headquarters.

Various committees and ad hoc groups are part of the new structure that advise and assist the Financial Services Policy Committee and the Information Technology Oversight Committee.

Therefore, the pyramid that Jack referred to is still present, but the "jello" has become much more pliable under the new structure. And it certainly is a more efficient way for the Fed to do business.

Monetary Policy

The structure for monetary policy decisions in the Fed is as follows:

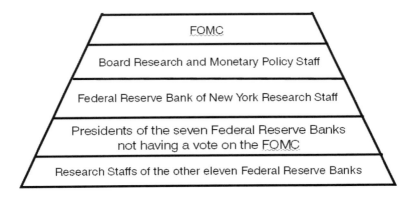

The twelve members of the FOMC make all decisions on monetary policy in the Fed. As mentioned earlier, the membership consists of the seven members of the Board of Governors, the president of the Federal Reserve Bank of New York, and four presidents of Federal Reserve Banks whose turn it is to sit on the FOMC as voting members.

The FOMC is supported by the Board of Governors' research and statistics staff and monetary policy staff; the Federal Reserve Bank of New York's research staff; the nonvoting presidents of the seven Federal Reserve Banks; and the research staffs of the banks. A total of 1,370 staff members are involved.

Each of the twelve members has a vote on the FOMC. By the time the FOMC votes on anything, consensus usually has been established because of the staff work and discussions within the Fed, and within the FOMC, that have preceded an FOMC vote.

The Fed chairman and the six Board members have seven of the twelve votes—thus they can control the FOMC. The Fed chairman is expected to provide the leadership. Rarely does the FOMC or the Board not support a chairman's position—but it has happened. In such a case, the chairman's vote is recorded with the minority votes—and this is not a good thing to happen to a Fed chairman. When it happened to Paul Volcker, he threatened to resign but was persuaded to remain as chairman.

Our economy is immense, and many things other than just monetary policy affect it. For example, in addition to fiscal policy—that is, what the rest of the government is doing—aberrations have significant effects, such as wars, actions of the OPEC cartel, etc.

In many cases, these other factors can moderate and even override the FOMC's actions on monetary policy. While the FOMC may be driving up interest rates to slow down the economy and the threat of inflationary forces, the rest of the Federal government might be setting record spending and deficit levels—thus fueling inflation and countering the FOMC's actions.

The Fed has access to enormous amounts of data. The financial industry and others are required by law to report regularly, in a timely manner, to the Fed and to other government agencies, such as the Department of Commerce. The Fed closely monitors all sectors of the economy through use of such information.

The objective of the FOMC in affecting monetary policy is to "promote effectively the goals of maximum employment, stable prices, and moderate long-term interest rates," according to *The Federal Reserve System: Proposes and Functions, 2005,* a Fed publication. Too much growth is harmful—as is too little growth. Too much inflation is harmful, and of course, so is deflation. A fully employed workforce includes about 3 percent of employable persons being unemployed because of movements between jobs, etc.

Fundamentally, there are three ways the FOMC can affect interest rates:

1. Change "reserve requirements," the amount that com-

mercial banks must retain on deposit with the Fed (or in vault cash). The Fed seldom does this.

2. Change the "discount rate," the interest rate that is charged to commercial banks for borrowings from the Fed. The Fed does this occasionally, and such changes are consistent with its targets for the "Fed funds" rate.

3. Buy and sell government securities from and to commercial banks and others in the financial industry through the Open Market Desk housed in the Federal Reserve Bank of New York. The Fed does this regularly, and uses this tool to affect the "Fed funds" rate, the interest rate that commercial banks charge one another for borrowings.

If the FOMC wants the Fed funds rate to increase, they will sell government securities to banks—thus removing from the banking system money that could be used for lending, and other purposes. The lesser amount of money available means banks must pay a higher interest rate on their borrowings from one another.

If the FOMC desires to reduce the Fed funds rate, they will buy government securities from banks, thus infusing funds into the banking system. A greater amount of money available for lending lowers the interest rate on their borrowings from one another.

The Fed also engages in "repurchase transactions" and "reverse repurchase transactions" to temporarily add to or subtract from money available in the banking system for lending purposes. In a repurchase transaction, the Fed accepts a security as collateral and lends money, for example, to a primary dealer, thus adding funds to the banking system. In a reverse purchase transaction, the Fed accepts a loan from a primary dealer, thus removing funds from the banking system, and collateralizes the loan with a security.

Monetary Aggregates

In the 1970s and 1980s, changes in the Fed's monetary aggregates—M1, M2, and M3—were often part of financial reporting on monetary policy. Although the Fed still publishes data on the monetary aggregates, these have become less important over time because of technical problems with their use as guides to or as explanations of Fed policy. (M1 includes currency in circulation, demand deposits, and NOW accounts; M2 includes all of M1 plus savings deposits and money market accounts; and M3 includes M2 plus large-value time deposits, money market accounts, repurchase agreements, and Eurodollars.)

As a related matter, I once got a big laugh at a "roasting" by stating that the individual involved had just returned from a Fed briefing on the aggregates and thought they were talking about rifles.

Jawboning

The Fed will also attempt to get changes in economic behavior by "jawboning." Arthur Burns used this tactic extensively with Congress and the White House in an attempt to drive down Federal government spending and the deficit. The Board members often give speeches, and some use these opportunities to attempt to elicit changes in behavior or to send out "signals" to various sectors of the economy. Most recently, Greenspan's "irrational exuberance" comment to the stock market was such a message.

Fed staff members also have opportunities to "jawbone" the banking industry.

The American Bankers Association and the Bank Administration Institute orchestrate many conventions and meetings for their banker constituency each year. Fed staffers are invited to be speakers at these functions—and they use the opportunities to update bankers on what the Fed is doing or thinking about doing. (Of course, they are careful not to get "in front" of the Board on any issue.)

By Fed policy, its staffers are prohibited from accepting any gratuities for these speaking engagements or reimbursement of expenditures. This is to preclude any Fed person from being "indebted" to the organizers of these functions, or to bankers whom they regulate. Thus, Fed speakers are "inexpensive" and in demand.

In the mid 1970s, I was a speaker at one of these banking conventions—and Ara Parseghian, the legendary Notre Dame football coach, was the keynote speaker. The night before the convention began, the sponsors of the convention hosted all speakers at a cocktail party. I attended and virtually all other speakers did also, including Parseghian.

I took the opportunity to introduce myself and asked him if he recalled who the opponent was when he coached his first football game for Northwestern University in 1956. (Parseghian was the head coach at Miami of Ohio, then at Northwestern, and then at Notre Dame. He beat Notre Dame a number of times when he was at Northwestern, and Notre Dame later hired him.)

He replied that the opponent was Iowa State, and that Northwestern won by one point, 14–13. I said, "You're looking at the quarterback who put up Iowa State's scores in that game." We had a nice chat.

Very few people know that in Ara Parseghian's first year at Northwestern, his freshman football team coach was Bo Schembechler, the legendary Michigan coach.

Foreign Currency Operations

Under its "foreign currency intervention operations," the Fed may buy and sell dollars in exchange for foreign currency. This is done under the direction of the FOMC through the Open Market Desk at the New York Fed, and is closely coordinated with the U.S. Treasury, which has overall responsibility for our nation's international financial policy. At the end of 2004, the Fed had $20 billion in foreign currency reserves for this purpose, and the Treasury had another $20 billion.

The FOMC's job is to orchestrate our nation's monetary policy, which affects our interest rates. When our interest rates rise, yields on dollar assets will be more attractive and this will lead to increases in the value of the dollar on the foreign exchanges. The stronger dollar will mean that our imports will cost less, and our exports will cost more to foreign purchasers. Conversely, when our interest rates fall, the dollar will lose value in the foreign exchange markets, making our imports cost more and our exports cost less. For example, we had significant downward pressures on the dollar when Fed funds traded at 1 percent in the early 2000s and, as a result, all interest rates in our economy were low.

Occasionally, and now more rarely than previously was the case prior to 1995, the FOMC will intervene to counter disorderly conditions in the exchange markets through the purchase and sale of foreign currencies. During periods when there is downward pressure on the dollar, the FOMC will sell foreign currencies and purchase dollars to absorb some of the pressure. Conversely, the FOMC may sell dollars and purchase foreign currencies to counter upward pressures on our dollar. Since 1995, the FOMC has intervened much less frequently than in the past. This is because the FOMC does not wish these interventions to be misinterpreted as a major focus of monetary policy. (However, the FOMC did intervene enough in 2005 to post losses of $2.7 billion, presumably in support of our soft dollar.)

Of course, factors other than just prevailing interest rates in a country determine the value of its currency in the foreign exchange markets. Otherwise, some third world countries with historical interest rate levels in the double digits would have the strongest currencies.

Lag Time

The problem that the FOMC faces is the "lag" time necessary for any of its actions to work its way into the economy.

For example, if the Fed funds rate goes up or down, eventually so do all other interest rates in the economy—short- and long-term ones, such as mortgage rates—because these are "pegged" off of the Fed funds rate. The lag time for this increase or decrease in interest rates to work its way into the economy and "be felt" has been estimated to be three months to 2.5 years or longer, depending upon circumstances and the economist you are talking to.

The reality is that when the FOMC initiates actions to raise or lower interest rates, it usually does so in a series of actions—that is, for example, increasing or lowering the Fed funds rate by a quarter to a half point a multiple number of times in a relatively short time period. The lag time necessary for each such action to work its way into the economy and "be felt" prevents the FOMC from knowing what the effect of its first action will be before it takes another action, and another, and another.

Monetary policy is not a science; it may not even be an art. The FOMC does not have the capability to fine-tune the economy—as some who have authored books on Fed Chairmen would lead you to believe.

When the FOMC takes any action, the best it can do is to judge and estimate what this action, and others it takes, will do to the economy. In essence, it's all over before they really know for certain what they did.

As a related matter, I was visiting the Federal Reserve Bank of San Francisco in the late 1970s and was approached by Milton Friedman, then the Nobel Laureate and Chairman Emeritus of the Finance Department at the University of Chicago. He was there to discuss economic matters with the Board of Directors of the Bank, as a consultant, and he learned that I was also visiting and was from the Board in Washington. He decided to take the opportunity to give me a message to take back to the Board of Governors.

He lectured me twenty to thirty minutes, and told me in no uncertain terms that the Board of Governors would do better "if they just put the numbers in a computer and let the computer make the decisions," and that "they just mess it up when they do it."

I thanked him for his message, and got to experience some of his feistiness firsthand.

Alibis and Repercussions

In the past, the Fed occasionally has made the argument—especially when times are bad—that it is not responsible for the high level of interest rates that usually accompany and contribute to a slowing economy. They have argued that they target the money supply and not interest rates, and that the latter are set by the market. I have heard this posed in various ways by at least two Fed chairmen.

Fundamental economics teaches you that whoever controls the supply of any product or service, controls the price. What is the price of money? Interest rates. If you control the supply of money in the economy, you control the price—interest rates.

Occasionally, things can get very difficult for a Fed chairman—particularly when the FOMC is in a "hawkish" mood and driving up interest rates in a petering-out economy.

Paul Volcker gets a lot of credit from the media, and from others, in holding to the gun and retaining high levels of interest rates for a prolonged period in the early mid-1980s in order to "wring out" double-digit inflation from our economy. (In hindsight, some Fed watchers have argued that he kept interest rate levels too high for about two years too long.)

If you have ever been in a country with rampant inflation, you know that Volcker did the right thing in ensuring that the embers of inflation were extinguished. However, that was not done without great cost.

I recall going to his office one morning during this time period of high interest rates, along with George Mitchell, to brief him on some matters. (George had retired from the Board, but was retained as a consultant on payments mechanism matters.)

In Volcker's outer office, where his secretary functioned, there was a five-foot-tall and twelve-foot-long pile of one-foot-long sections of two-by-fours. The housing industry, virtually put out of business by the crusade to eradicate inflation, had a nationwide campaign going in which they mailed to Volcker these one-foot-long sections of two-by-fours. Each morning, the postal system would deliver a large pile to Volcker's office—which would then be removed to the basement. This went on for quite some time.

During this same time period, the trucking industry used their vehicles to "choke" the metropolitan area of Washington, D.C., in a protest over the unrelenting efforts of the FOMC to eradicate inflation. They literally stopped traffic by parking their vehicles on the highways and streets in such a way as to prevent traffic from moving.

Countless small businessmen, entrepreneurs, and blue-collar workers were brought to their knees because of this unrelenting inflation war. So were the S&Ls. (See Chapter 8.) The costs were phenomenal, and the pressures on the Fed, and especially its chairman, were significant. But inflation was defeated.

Volatile Market

It is about this time that I had left the Fed and became the CEO of a central bank for credit unions, U.S. Central Credit Union. We were a unique organization—because we had grown to a level wherein we became one of the largest sellers of Fed funds in the nation. Each day, we were investing $8–9 billion into the Fed funds market.

I recall the price of Fed funds fluctuating from 2 percent to 32 percent within one business day during this time period. Normally, the range of fluctuations in the price of Fed funds within any business day is considerably smaller—on the order of .5–1 percent, and even smaller in low-interest-rate environments. Talk about a financial management problem. Timing your sales was critically important. If you did a bad job, you left a lot of money on the table. Fortunately, we developed a strategy that enabled us to benefit from such wide swings in the Fed funds rate. And being one of the largest sellers of Fed funds in the nation, we had to be certain that we were not driving down the price of Fed funds by what we did. This, of course, would work to our detriment.

Others were not as fortunate. During the period of this volatile Fed funds market, we purchased funds daily from the Bank of America, at that time the largest commercial bank in the nation, and arbitraged such funds for profit in the New York market. This went on for a period of several months, but then came to an abrupt halt.

A money trader in New York, attempting to ingratiate himself with the Fed funds money manager for the Bank of America, spilled the beans. The young lady at the Bank of America refused to do business with us thereafter. But we took pride in getting into the pockets of the largest bank in the country for a considerable period of time.

Also during this time period, John Perkins, then president of Continental Illinois, made an appointment to see me at my U.S. Central office in Overland Park, Kansas. The purpose of his visit, as I subsequently learned, was to convince me of the creditworthiness of his bank.

We had removed his bank from our approved list sometime earlier. Continental Illinois obviously was having difficulty funding itself in the market and was into the Fed's "discount window"—and thus the reason for his visit. U.S. Central was indeed one of the largest sellers of Fed Funds in the nation, and if he could get us to again sell funds to his bank, it would be very helpful to them.

Financial institutions eligible to borrow at the Fed's "discount window" normally will look to the market for their borrowings, rather than using the Fed's window. And if they do use it, they are encouraged by the Fed to be in and out of it quickly. In essence, the Fed is the "lender of last resort." Healthy institutions are able to rely upon the market for their borrowings, and the Fed knows this and so does the market. (Recently, the Fed has become somewhat more encouraging to healthy financial institutions and their access to the window, and especially in reaction to the recession triggered by the subprime problem.)

The discount window is very helpful to the Fed when it is attempting to stabilize and reassure the financial markets, such as immediately following a disaster, as in the case of 9/11 and the subprime mess. The Fed lets the market know that liquidity will be available to those who need it, and this has a significant calming effect on the market.

But getting back to Perkins, after some initial small talk, he began to address the internal bank reports that he brought along with him. I interrupted him and told him that we just could not sell funds to his bank. He left my office but returned the following week, again seeking to purchase Fed funds from us. I knew then that the situation had become untenable for the bank, and the Federal regulator interceded in the operation and in the management of the bank shortly thereafter.

Whenever problems surfaced for a financial institution on our approved list, we immediately ceased doing business with them. I recall at that time, Texas Commerce moving from being an A rated bank to a "B+"-rated bank. I instructed my staff to stop doing business with Texas Commerce and some objected, stating that B+ was still a high rating. My answer was, "Until we fully understand what's going on, they are off the list as of now." Within a short period of time thereafter, the rating on Texas Commerce spiraled downward and their situation became critical, resulting in their demise.

U.S. Central was, at the time, perhaps the most risk-averse financial institution in the world. Among other matters, we duration-matched our assets and liabilities, and only dealt with the most creditworthy organizations in the world. Therefore, as the S&L industry was crumbling, and some big banks in this country were experiencing major problems, we enjoyed the highest debt ratings available from Moody's and from Standard and Poor's. This opened many opportunities to us.

For example, Merrill Lynch at that time was very much interested in adding liquidity to its balance sheet at the year's end. Their officers approached us, and we agreed to engage in a year-end repurchase transaction with them. They sold to us a large dollar amount of government securities between Christmas and New Year's, which they agreed to buy back shortly after the start of the New Year. This enabled them to show substantially more liquidity on their balance sheet at the close of the calendar year, December 31. We, in turn, enjoyed an interest rate on our cash loan to them—which was fully collateralized, secured, and perfected (which meant we had legal possession of the securities and could sell them if there was a default by Merrill Lynch)—that was two or three times the effective Fed funds rate for the period. It was very profitable for us to accommodate Merrill Lynch in this manner for a number of years.

Unfortunately, over the years, U.S. Central began to assume more risk and became a casualty of the subprime problem and was recently put in conservatorship by its regulator, the National Credit Union Administration.

Challenges to Independence

During times when the Fed creates enormous pressures on our economy—as it did during Volcker's tenure—the challenges to the Fed's independence surface with a vengeance. Some in Congress lead this charge, claiming, among other matters, that so few nonelected officials should not have the power and authority to inflict such heavy damage on so many. This is often accompanied by various proposals to abate the Fed's free hand in administering such punitive economic action.

It is then that the Fed "circles the wagons," so to speak. The entire Federal Reserve System rises to the occasion. Soon an outpouring of support for the continued independence of the Fed is heard from virtually all financial sectors of the economy, led, of course, by Wall Street, and the threat is extinguished.

5

World's Money Mover

Perhaps the best kept secret of the Fed is that it is the world's money mover. Our central bank is the facility through which payors and payees around the world settle their daily business (and government) transactions. Every 3.17 business days, a dollar amount equal to our gross domestic product (GDP) is moved and settled through the Fed. Every 11.18 business days, a dollar amount equal to the world's GDP is moved and settled through the Fed.

(Our GDP is the total value of all goods and services produced in our nation in one year; the world's GDP is the total value of all goods and services produced in the world in one year.)

Let's put this tremendous dollar volume in perspective so that we can better understand it.

GDP and the Soft Dollar

How large is our GDP?

In 2002 it was larger than the combined GDPs of the next five most-prosperous nations in the world: Japan, Germany, the United Kingdom, France, and China. We had 32.3 percent of the world's wealth and they had 31.8 percent. Our GDP was $10.4 trillion and those five countries had a combined GDP, in dollar equivalents, of $10.25 trillion, while the world's was $32.3 trillion (see Chart 2). Thus our GDP was equal to one-third of the world's, and so was theirs. Jointly, we held two-thirds of the wealth on this planet.

In 2004, our GDP increased to $11.71 trillion, the combined GDPs of those five countries, in dollar equivalents, increased to $13.46 trillion, while the world's rose to $41.3 trillion. Our percentage of the world's GDP decreased to 28.4 percent and theirs increased to 32.62 percent. But this "shifting" in percentages was due primarily to the decrease in the value of our dollar versus the yen, pound, and euro dollar—which inflated their GDPs since these were recorded as dollar equivalents. Only one of the five countries actually experienced a dramatic increase in GDP—China's increased by almost 56 percent from 2002 to 2004, according to the World Bank's numbers, and by policy, China sets a fixed exchange rate on its currency versus the dollar. So, their GDP growth was real. The other four countries actually experienced a GDP growth rate less than our 12.4 percent from 2002 to 2004—after adjusting for the inflationary effect of the weaker dollar on their currencies.

GDP Rankings, 2002

Ranking	Economy	(millions of US dollars)
1	United States	10,416,818
2	Japan	3,978,782
3	Germany	1,976,240
4	United Kingdom	1,552,437
5	France	1,409,604[a]
6	China	1,237,145
7	Italy	1,180,921
8	Canada	715,692
9	Spain	649,792
10	Mexico	637,205
11	India	515,012
12	Korea, Rep.	476,690
13	Brazil	452,387
14	Netherlands	413,741
15	Australia	410,590
16	Russian Federation	346,520
17	Switzerland	268,041
18	Belgium	247,634

19	Sweden	229,772
20	Austria	202,954
21	Norway	189,436
22	Poland	187,660
23	Saudi Arabia	*186,409*
24	Turkey	182,848
25	Denmark	174,798
26	Indonesia	172,911
27	Hong Kong, China	161,532
28	Greece	132,834
29	Finland	130,797
30	Thailand	126,407
31	Portugal	121,291
32	Ireland	119,916
33	Israel	*110,386*
34	Iran, Islamic Rep.	107,522
35	South Africa	104,235
36	Argentina	102,191
37	Malaysia	95,157
38	Venezuela	94,340
39	Egypt, Arab Rep.	89,845
40	Singapore	86,969
41	Colombia	82,194
42	Philippines	77,076
43	Czech Republic	69,590
44	Puerto Rico	67,897
45	Hungary	65,843
46	Chile	64,154
47	Pakistan	60,521
48	New Zealand	58,178
49	Peru	56,901
50	Algeria	55,666
51	Bangladesh	47,328
52	Romania	44,428
53	Nigeria	43,540
54	Ukraine	41,380
55	Morocco	37,263
56	Vietnam	35,110
57	Libya	34,137
58	Kuwait	32,791
59	Ecuador	24,347
60	Kazakhstan	24,205
61	Slovak Republic	23,700
62	Guatemala	23,252
63	Croatia	22,421

GDP Rankings, 2002

Ranking	Economy	(millions of US dollars)
64	Syrian Arab Republic	21,872
65	Dominican Republic	21,285
66	Tunisia	21,169
67	Slovenia	21,108
68	Oman	20,073
69	Luxembourg	20,062
70	Lebanon	17,294
71	Costa Rica	16,887
72	Qatar	16,454
73	Sri Lanka	16,373
74	Bulgaria	15,608
75	Serbia and Montenegro	15,555
76	Belarus	14,304
77	El Salvador	14,287
78	Lithuania	13,796
79	Sudan	13,450
80	Uruguay	12,325
81	Panama	12,296
82	Kenya	12,140
83	Côte d'Ivoire	11,717
84	Angola	11.380
85	Yemen, Rep.	10,395
86	Uzbekistan	9,713
87	Tanzania	9,383[b]
88	Trinidad and Tobago	9,372
89	Jordan	9,296
90	Cyprus	*9,131*
91	Cameroon	9,060
92	Iceland	8,608
93	Latvia	8,406
94	Zimbabwe	8,304
95	Jamaica	8,001
96	Bahrain	7,935
97	Bolivia	7,678
98	Turkmenistan	7,672
99	Honduras	6,594
100	Estonia	6,413
101	Macao, China	*6,199*
102	Azerbaijan	6.090
103	Ghana	6,021
104	Ethiopia	5,989
105	Uganda	5,866
106	Congo, Dem. Rep.	5,704
107	Nepal	5,493
108	Paraguay	5,389

109	Bosnia and Herzegovina	5,249
110	Botswana	5,188
111	Gabon	4,971
112	Senegal	4,940
113	Bahamas	4,818
114	Albania	4,695
115	Mauritius	4,532
116	Madagascar	4,514
117	Mozambique	3,920
118	Macedonia, FYR	3,712
119	Zambia	3,683
120	Cambodia	3,677
121	Malta	3,614
122	Haiti	3,590
123	French Polynesia	3,448
124	Georgia	3,324
125	Guinea	3,174
126	Mali	3,163

GDP Rankings, 2002

Ranking	Economy	(millions of US dollars)
127	West Bank and Gaza	3,015
128	Congo, Rep.	3,014
129	Burkina Paso	2,839
130	Papua New Guinea	2,793
131	Namibia	2,793
132	Barbados	2,757
133	Benin	2,630
134	New Caledonia	2,682
135	Armenia	2,367
136	Equatorial Guinea	2,173
137	Niger	2,170
138	Chad	1,935
139	Malawi	1,880
140	Fiji	1,878
141	Rwanda	1,736
142	Lao PDR	1,680
143	Kyrgyz Republic	1,632
144	Moldova	1,621
145	Togo	1,384
146	Mongolia	1,262
147	Tajikistan	1,208
148	Swaziland	1,177
149	Central African Republic	1,075
150	Mauritania	983
151	Suriname	895

152	Belize	843
153	Sierra Leone	789
154	Lesotho	730
155	Burundi	719
156	Antigua and Barbuda	710
157	Guyana	710
158	St. Lucia	660
159	Cape Verde	631
160	Seychelles	630
161	Maldives	618
162	Djibouti	597
163	Bhutan	594
164	Eritrea	582
165	Liberia	564
166	Grenada	414
167	Gambia, The	388
168	Timor-Leste	388
169	St. Vincent and the Grenadines	361
170	St. Kitts and Nevis	340
171	Samoa	261
172	Comoros	256
173	Dominica	254
174	Solomon Islands	240
175	Vanuatu	234
176	Micronesia, Fed. Sts.	232
177	Guinea-Bissau	216
178	Tonga	136
179	Palau	130
180	Marshall Islands	108
181	Sao Tome and Principe	50
182	Kiribati	44

	Afghanistan	"
	American Samoa	"
	Andorra	"
	Aruba	"
	Bermuda	"
	Brunei	"

67

GDP Rankings, 2002

Ranking	Economy	(millions of US dollars)
	Cayman Islands	"
	Channel Islands	"
	Cuba	"
	Faeroe Islands	"
	Greenland	"
	Guam	"
	Iraq	"
	Isle of Man	"
	Korea, Dem. Rep.	"
	Liechtenstein	"
	Mayotte	"
	Monaco	"
	Myanmar	"
	Netherlands Antilles	"
	Nicaragua	"
	Northern Mariana Islands	"
	San Marino	"
	Somalia	"
	United Arab Emirates	"
	Virgin Islands (U.S.)	"
	World	**32,353,480**
	Low income	1,130,469
	Middle Income	5,127,124
	Lower middle Income	3,400,282
	Upper middle income	1,702,097
	Low and middle income	6,256,339
	East Asia and Pacific	1,802.082
	Europe and Central Asia	1,135,666
	Latin America and Caribbean	1,672,945
	Middle East and North Africa	693,526
	South Asia	
	Sub-Saharan Africa	318,631
	High income	25,991,523
	European Monetary Union	6,605,786

"Not available.
Note: Rankings include only these economies With confirmed GDP
estimates. Figures in italics are the most recent estimate from 2001 or
2000.

a. Data include the French overseas departments of French Guiana, Guadeloupe, Martinique, and Réunion.
b. Data refer to mainland Tanzania only.l
Source: World Development indicators database, World Bank, July 2003.

Our GDP today of $14 trillion is gargantuan as compared to the other countries of the world, even given our ongoing problems. This enables us to accommodate the type of reactions necessary to deal with the problems emanating from subprime more easily, including our nation's worst recession since the Great Depression. Our commitment of over $10 trillion to reestablish liquidity in our capital markets, and for stimulating fiscal policies to support our financial system, is a good example.

Unfortunately, our national debt has ballooned to $12 trillion, and the Congressional Budget Office projects our debt to double in the next five years and triple in ten years. This will cause us other problems in the future.

A Quadrillion Dollars

And what happened to the amount of money that the Fed moved during this "shifting" in the GDP numbers due to devaluation of our dollar?

In 2003, the Fed moved and settled $742 trillion. In 2005, that increased to $923.7 trillion. That was a dollar amount equal to seventy-nine times our GDP and twenty-two times the world's GDP.

In 2006, the Fed exceeded the moving of $1,000 trillion, also known as a quadrillion dollars. That's a one followed by fifteen zeros.

This megadollar volume of funds movement and settlement occurs because of the payment services that the Fed provides to domestic and international commercial banks, to thrifts, including savings and loans, mutual savings banks and credit unions, to the Federal government, primarily the U S.

69

Treasury, and to certain Wall Street organizations. These payment services include:

1. Fed wire (the wire transfer of funds and securities);
2. National Settlement Services (NSS) to organizations of financial institutions;
3. check clearing and settlement;
4. Automated clearing house ((ACH);
5. currency and coin; and
6. fiscal agency (supporting government organizations).

The majority of the megadollar volume emanates from Fed wire and the Fed's National Settlement Services. In 2005, for example, the Fed effected 132.5 million wire transfers having a value of $518.6 trillion, 22.4 million security transfers having a value of $369 trillion, and 440,000 settlements through NSS for check-clearing associations, credit card processors, and Chips, having a value of $5.7 trillion. The Fed also cleared and settled $30.7 trillion in check and ACH payments. These volumes have grown since then.

Importance of the Fed

How important is the Fed to our nation's, and the world's, financial stability and well-being?

Is it possible for the Fed to make an error or two (or more) in effecting our nation's monetary policy without bringing down the world's economic system?

Of course it is, as the Fed has erred many times. Virtually every Fed chairman and the FOMC under their leadership have made mistakes—some more severe than others. They will be the first to admit that, and the professional "Fed watchers" will be the first to corroborate that. As a result, the world's economic systems may have suffered some bumps and bruises, but had no trouble surviving.

Is it possible for the Fed to become totally dysfunctional for even one day in moving funds and settling dollars for whatever reason—human error, hardware malfunction, criminal penetration, etc.—without creating worldwide liquidity and other crises?

If the Fed became totally dysfunctional for even one day, the impact of such would be felt throughout this nation's and the world's economies. If it were a nonrecoverable situation, it would be catastrophic. In any event, the prospects for catastrophe are far greater than that emanating from errors in conducting monetary policy.

"Good Funds"

In addition to Fed wire, there is one banking type wire system, known as Chips, operated by the private sector.

But, this is a wire system in name only, because reliance must be placed upon the Fed for the actual transfer of dollars. The information pertinent to the wire transfer moves on this network from the originating bank to the receiving bank. The actual dollars, however, are transferred from the originator to the receiver on Fed books, namely, through the reserve accounts of the banks involved in the transfer. Settlement for Chips wire transfers occurs at the end of the business day on Fed books. Almost all of the dollar volume in the Fed's National Settlement Services emanates from Chips settlement, now over $1.36 trillion daily.

Thus, Fed wire is the only "good funds" wire transfer network on the planet, meaning that the dollars associated with a wire transfer move simultaneously with the information.

For example, when the originating bank hits the "send" key on its Fed terminal, the information pertinent to the transfer is accepted by the Fed and that bank's reserve account is debited for the dollar amount, simultaneously. Likewise, at the moment the Fed delivers the wire transfer information to the receiving bank's terminal, that bank's reserve account is credited with the dollar amount. The wire transfer can vary from being completed instantaneously, to a time delay of a maximum of two to three minutes during high-volume time periods.

Thus, if you are a receiver of funds, you want the sender to use Fed Wire so that you have immediate access to the funds. If you are a sender, you are motivated to use Chips because you have use of the funds until the end of the business day, at which time the settlement occurs on Fed books and the amount is deducted from your reserve account. Most parties to wire transfers specify the network to be used at the outset to avoid problems.

There is a nuance associated with how financial institutions use Fed wire that works to the detriment of its customers, particularly consumers. Every financial institution using Fed wire prefers to wait until it receives funds before sending funds. It attempts to avoid overdrawing its reserve account or clearing balances—because the Fed may impose penalties for daylight overdrafts.

If you are a consumer wiring funds, normally such funds are already in your account. But question your financial institution the next time it wires funds on your behalf. You will find, invariably, that funds will be wired on your behalf just prior to the closing of Fed wire, which, for third-party transfers, occurs at 6:00 P.M., eastern time. Since the funds that you are wiring are already in your account, there is no valid reason to delay the transfer. But financial institutions do so. In essence they are using your funds to maintain a required positive balance in their account with the Fed—and they delay in making the wire transfer on your behalf until they receive their incoming wires expected for that day.

If you are making an investment by having funds wired to, for example, a mutual fund or a broker, the stock market closes at 4 P.M. eastern—and you just missed that day's cutoff. Your investment will be effected the following day, and this can be to your detriment.

Enabler of Good Funds

The reason that the Fed has the only "good funds" wire transfer system on the planet is because it has custody of the holding of the reserves that financial depository institutions must maintain with the Fed.

Reserve requirements are specified as a percentage of the amount deposited in transaction accounts (demand and certain time accounts) in our nation's financial depository institutions. For example, in 2005, reserve requirements were as follows:

> Zero for those depositories that had less than $7.8 million in transaction accounts
> Three percent for those with between $7.8 and $48.3 million in transaction accounts
> 10 percent of transaction accounts over $48.3 million.

The level of reserve requirements has fallen appreciably since the early 1990s because of the widespread use of "sweep" accounts in financial institutions. The funds in a business or consumer checking account that are in excess of what is needed to cover today's items that arrive for payment are "swept' into a special-purpose money market account paying a higher rate of interest. Since the money market account is not a transaction account, the financial institution does not include its deposits in such accounts in calculating its reserve requirements. At year's end, 2005, $10.4 billion was deposited in reserve accounts with the Fed. By comparison, there was $37 billion in such accounts at year's end in 1990. Today, there is $800 billion in such accounts, representing a temporary increase due to the Fed's expanding its balance sheet to $2 trillion to stabilize the financial markets.

What is a reserve account?

In essence, it is a bank account that operates much like your checking account. Throughout the business day, financial institutions receive funds from many sources, and also disburse funds to many different parties, including businesses, banks, and individuals. All such receipts and disbursements are made to and from the institution's reserve account. Thus, not only does the account hold required reserves, it also serves as a transaction account into which all of the institution's receipts go and from which all of its disbursements are made.

Originally, only member banks of the Federal Reserve had reserve accounts and were subject to maintaining reserves. This was a cost they had to bare that other financial depositories avoided since reserves were "sterile," i.e., they earned no interest. But such member banks also were the only financial depositories that had direct access to Fed services. All other financial depositories accessed Fed services through a member bank of the Fed—thus paying a fee to the member bank that made up for the member bank's lost income from its sterile reserves.

The Monetary Control Act of 1980 changed all of that. It made reserve requirements mandatory for all depository institutions. And it gave all financial depositories direct access to Fed services.

Through Fedwire, for example, a financial institution can receive funds from virtually any organization in the world, domestic or foreign, and send funds to any organization. This is how the system works.

When the institution wishes to send funds, it communicates the wire transfer instructions to the Fed. The Fed then acts on these instructions, by debiting the reserve account of the sending institution and forwarding the instructions to the Reserve Bank serving the receiving institution. There, the Fed credits the reserve account of the receiving institution, and communicates the relevant data to that institution. Thus, money moves out of one institution's reserve account and into another's instantaneously. (Such wire transfers can be on behalf of the customers of the institutions, or to settle their own business with one another.)

Without reserve accounts, each institution would have to have an account with every other institution with which it conducts business. Not only would this be inefficient and costly, but for the larger money center banks—such as Citibank—it would be impossible since the bank may do business with virtually any bank, business organization, or government entity in the world. This is why Chips settles their wire transfers through the Fed at the end of the business day. The Fed has the reserve accounts of its Chips member banks, which makes these settlements possible and pain free. Reserve accounts provide our nation's depositories with access to the financial world.

It is doubtful that the founders of the Fed could have visualized how tremendously important reserve accounts have become to our commercial bankers, mutual savings banks, S&Ls, credit unions, and to the Fed. On December 23, 1913, when President Woodrow Wilson signed the Federal Reserve Act establishing the Federal Reserve System, reserve accounts were intended as a "safety" measure in banking.

They have since become the primary transaction account for our financial depositories, and have placed the Fed at the locus of activity in banking. Since every transaction in which a depository participates that involves the transfer of money from one party to another is settled through its reserve account, and since the Fed maintains these accounts, the Fed has a virtual "real-time" window into commercial banking.

Reserve Requirements

Under the Fed's rules, reserve requirements can be averaged over a certain period of time for its member banks. What does this mean?

Let's assume that the reserve requirement for a bank is $100. If the bank desires, it can hold $700 in its reserve account for one day, and $0 for the next six days.

Now remember that this account is also the bank's primary transaction account. So during any given day, substantially more funds are in the account from time to time, depending upon its transactional requirements. The bank will use these funds to settle its transactions, perhaps sell excess funds to another bank, but at the close of the business day, it must have at least $100 in its reserve account each day, or on average each day.

The Fed imputes earnings to balances maintained in reserve accounts, and such earnings are used by member commercial banks to pay for Fed services that are used. If these imputed earnings are not sufficient to cover the cost of services used, the Fed will charge fees for the excess.

Clearing Balances

Not all financial depositories have reserve accounts. Some don't have them because their transaction account balances are less than $7 million in aggregate. Others don't have them because their "vault" cash fulfills their reserve requirements. These institutions can hold "clearing balances" with the Fed, and such accounts are the primary transaction accounts of these institutions. These accounts were established by the Fed in the early 1980s to provide nonmember financial institutions with direct access to Fed services. Previous to the establishment of such accounts, Fed nonmember institutions had to access Fed services through a member commercial bank.

Minimum balance requirements are required by the Fed on such accounts, which must be maintained on deposit with the Fed. At the year's end, 2005, required clearing balances of $8.7 billion were on deposit with the Fed. This amount was down from a high of $11.8 billion in these accounts in 2003. The Fed imputes earnings on such balances as well, which are used to pay for the Fed services these institutions utilize. Also, the Fed imposes fees when imputed earnings are not sufficient to pay for all Fed services used.

Historical Perspective

Fedwire has undergone revolutionary changes over the past thirty-plus years. It is interesting to review the changes, starting in the early 1970s.

Arthur Burns was the chairman, and his predecessor, William McChesney Martin, did not convey to him a sophisticated wire system, nor one that was capable of meeting even minimal security requirements.

Now I'm not going to tell you that Burns was a computer expert or a communications technician. But I will tell you that he was the most intelligent human being that I have ever met, and could quickly get to the "heart" of an issue without knowing too much about it. And he had a Board member by the name of George Mitchell, who later became his vice chairman, and who was the nation's biggest proponent of modernizing this country's payments mechanism.

Burns appointed Mitchell as chairman of the Board's Committee on the Payments Mechanism. Mitchell hit the street running full speed—utilizing the Fed's resources to the fullest, including the pyramid structure of solving nationwide problems in the Fed (discussed earlier). Fedwire is the first area he emphasized—and not without reason, as you will see.

As chairman of the Board's Committee on the Payments Mechanism, Mitchell, in addition to other Board members, saw to it that Ernie Baughman, first vice president of the Chicago Fed, and Willis Winn, president of the Cleveland Fed, were also on the committee. This gave him a direct link to the resources of the Conferences of First Vice Presidents and Presidents, and to the pyramid structure of getting things done. George would "light the fire" under anyone not moving rapidly enough to suit his needs.

I recall him once saying to me, "Jim, get Bob in here for lunch. He appears to need a kick in the ass to get him moving on getting his RCPC up and running." So we had lunch with Bob, and he got the message. That's how George worked.

Bulls-eye

As a related matter, I was hired by the Board in the early 1970s because of my background with the Navy's Bulls-eye Project. At the time I was a lieutenant commander in the Naval Security Group, known as the "cryptologists" of the Navy. I was in the Ph.D. program at American University along with a fellow by the name of Warren Minami, a Board officer in the Computer Division. He alerted Jim Vining, an officer in the Division of Federal Reserve Bank Operations, about my background and desire to leave the Navy, and he hired me. He (actually, we jointly) then hired a communications networking specialist from the Control Data Corporation, Brian Carey, who would later prove to be one of the best networking and computer guys in the nation.

Vining, Carey, and Minami are three people who used the Fed as a stepping stone to better things. Vining joined the Union Planters Bank in Memphis and subsequently opened a securities brokerage firm and has been managing partner of Vining and Sparks, IBG, also in Memphis, since its start-up. (His firm bought none of the subprime backed securities and thus avoided the problems that our megabanks confronted, as discussed in chapter 11.) Carey became a highly paid and in-demand consultant. Minami became an executive with the World Bank. The three are indeed very bright and successful people.

The Bulls-eye Project in the Navy was going on at the same time as the Polaris Project—the latter, to develop a nuclear submarine missile launching system. It is interesting to note that Bulls-eye was the top-priority project in the Department of Defense (DOD) and Polaris was second.

The Bulls-eye Project automated the Navy's High Frequency Direction Finding (HFDF) network. The hardware and software used to facilitate automation, including communication, was state of the art at the time. Thus, the reason for the Fed's interest in me.

Briefly, the Navy had a number of HFDF networks in the

Pacific and the Atlantic. The stations in each network were thousands of miles apart. This is what each network did.

A target was identified through communications-intercept techniques and the network was alerted. Each station in the network took a bearing to the target. The spot at which the bearings from all the stations in the network intersected pinpointed the location of the target.

HFDF networks were used to plot and track, for example, Soviet submarines and surface vessels, and others as well.

The networks were also used to track aircraft that were making transoceanic flights. Transponders on the aircraft emitted a signal, and the stations in the network took bearings on that signal, periodically, until the aircraft reached its destination. Thus, the aircraft's location was verified throughout its flight. Today, all of these functions are performed by satellite technology.

Let's now take a look at Fedwire in the early 1970s. You will see what Mitchell saw—and recognize why its improvement became top priority with him.

Early 1970s

A woman called Helen worked in the Federal Reserve Bank of Chicago's wire transfer department. She was one of about 250 people who took telephone calls from the 3,200 commercial banks that were part of the seventh Fed District's field of membership, located throughout Illinois and adjoining states.

On Helen's desk was a telephone, a pad containing the forms that were used to record wire instructions, a cylinder containing ballpoint pens, and an "out" basket. All 250 desks were similarly equipped. All telephone calls were recorded.

A commercial bank wishing to wire transfer funds dialed a designated number at the Chicago Fed and was placed in a telephone queue, and the queue was serviced on a first-in, first-answered basis.

Each of the approximately 250 people in the Fed's phone

input area would connect to the next bank in the queue and accept its wire transfer instructions. These would be written on to the proper form and then the Fed phone operator would disconnect and pick up the next commercial bank in the queue.

The completed wire transfer forms were placed in an "out" basket, and these were emptied periodically, and the wire transfers were processed.

Processing involved transferring the information from the form to a five level paper tape, which was accomplished by the data input clerical staff. A keyboard, similar to a typewriter's, was used for this purpose. However, the stroke of a key did not result in a letter or a number being printed on to a piece of paper; it resulted in a letter or a number being punched into a five-level paper tape in a sequence that could be interpreted by a communications transmitter.

The paper tape was then inserted into the proper communications transmitter so that the wire transfer could be sent to the Federal Reserve Bank serving the recipient commercial bank. That Federal Reserve Bank's communications receiver would punch out a five-level paper tape containing the information pertinent to the wire transfer. That paper tape would then be inserted into a printer, and the holes in the tape would be translated into alphabetic and numeric characters, thus presenting the wire transfer instructions into a readable form so that it could be processed by the receiving Federal Reserve Bank.

Of course the reserve account of the sending bank was debited for the amount of the transfer concurrent with processing, and the reserve account of the receiving bank was credited for the amount as it was received.

Fraud

My first assignment in the Fed was working with the task force and the subcommittee assigned to improve the security of Fedwire. I was one of the Board representatives, along with

Jim Vining and Brian Carey. Others from Fed Banks and branches were also part of the group, including Howard Crumb of the New York Fed, who chaired the subcommittee.

As part of this process, we consulted with the National Security Agency (NSA), the Central Intelligence Agency (CIA), and the Federal Bureau of Investigation (FBI)—and they were very helpful and cooperative.

The NSA and the CIA were particularly helpful in educating us on the vulnerabilities of using telephone lines. Intercept of such communication, both vocal and when telephone lines are used as a data link, was easily accomplished.

The Fed, at that time, was vulnerable because voice telephone input and dial-up telephone data links were used extensively in Fedwire.

They also educated us on the vulnerabilities of dedicated "hard wire" communication links, which were also used in Fedwire, particularly between Fed offices, and between Fed offices and money center banks.

The FBI provided us with information on "white collar" crime that had been successfully perpetrated against the commercial banking industry's wire operations. This information became prophetic for us, as I will note.

We did numerous on-site analyses at Fed offices and at member commercial banks. The vulnerabilities that were found in Fedwire were staggering. Frankly, it was just by luck that Fedwire hadn't been penetrated. You didn't even have to be a very smart person to successfully do so. Let me give you the best example of the vulnerability.

One of the Fed offices that we analyzed was the Federal Reserve Bank of Chicago—chosen because it had the largest number of "endpoints" to serve, 3,200 member banks.

I walked into the middle of their telephone input section, where, as described earlier, 250 people were accepting wire transfer instructions from a telephone queue based on first call in, first call served.

Helen is one of the people I spoke to. We had a brief discussion, and ascertained that whenever she took a call from the queue, any one of the 3,200 banks that the Chicago Fed served could be on the other end of the line.

The calling bank was in the queue because it desired to make a wire transfer of funds. When Helen, a Fed operator, connected with the calling bank, it provided:

1. The calling bank's name and ABA number (a unique number identifying the bank);
2. the receiving bank's name, city and/or state location, and its ABA number;
3. the third-party information, such as, for "further credit to the account of John Doe, account number 12345";
4. the dollar amount of the transfer; and
5. the date.

I asked Helen a simple question, "How do you know that it is actually the bank calling, and not someone else claiming to be the bank?"

Helen thought for a moment and said, "I recognize the voice."

I said, "But Helen, how could you possibly recognize 3,200 voices, because when you take the next caller in the queue, it could be any one of 3,200 different banks on the line."

Helen smiled and said, "You're right. I really don't know it's the bank, but I assume it is, because they know the telephone procedure."

So anyone who could learn of the proper telephone procedure (steps one to five above) could input a wire into Fedwire. All a person had to do was go to its bank, order a valid wire transfer, note the information asked for, and that person had the telephone procedures needed.

Anyone who worked in banking would know these procedures. And anyone who dated a person working in a bank's wire operations could easily obtain the procedures.

As a matter of fact, the FBI files described such cases, where men sought out and dated women working in wire rooms of banks, to obtain the necessary information and procedures to fraudulently execute wire transfers.

Some women even became accomplices in the interest of retaining relationships.

In one case, a man sought out and began dating a woman who worked in the wire room of a bank in New Jersey. That bank used a correspondent bank in New York for its wire transfer services. (A correspondent bank sells its services to other banks.)

The man's accomplices opened a bank account with a California bank in the name of a concocted business. They told the bank that the business was expanding to the West Coast, and that shortly they would begin to receive large dollar amount wire transfers to provide funds for start-up costs. Thus, when funds came into the account and were removed, it would not be suspicious.

Then the man convinced the woman to input a $4 million fraudulent wire, which she did. She gave the instructions for the wire to her bank's correspondent bank in New York, which then wired the funds to the account of the nonexistent business on behalf of the New Jersey bank.

To make matters worse, both the New Jersey bank and its correspondent bank in New York were thirty days or more in arrears in balancing and accounting for their daily wire transfer activity.

By the time the New Jersey and New York banks noticed the $4 million disparity, the money was gone, and so were the man and his accomplices. Subsequently, two accomplices were apprehended, and the man remained "at large" at the time of the report.

Close Call

Nationwide, the great majority of wire transfers over the Fedwire in the 1970s were inputted via telephone instructions. Thus, this vulnerability existed at every Fed office. Money was there for the taking. All you needed was some simple and straightforward telephone protocol.

Now think of this. This is Fedwire, the "guts" of the world's funds movement and settlement system, handling a dollar volume each year that is seventy-nine times greater than our GDP and twenty-two times the GDP of the world—and subject to the most basic and elementary form of penetration and fraud.

The Task Force and Subcommittee on Wire Security prepared its final report, including the means of securing the network, and the recommendations went up through the pyramid to the Board of Governors, where they were approved as policy.

Many changes were implemented, including end-of-day close-out and balancing procedures, and hardware and software enhancements. In essence, a "security net" was placed around Fedwire.

The temporary solution to the telephone input vulnerability was a simple two-way authentication system. Two copies of a list of four character codes, randomly generated, were prepared for each member bank using telephone inputting. A unique list was prepared for each bank. The Fed office had one copy and the member bank had the other.

Prior to accepting wire transfer instructions, the member bank had to give the Fed telephone operator the next code in sequence, and then that code was deleted from both lists. The lists were secured at the Fed office and at the bank.

The permanent solution was to eliminate telephone inputs and to install hard-wired terminal hookups, or computer-to-computer connections, between Fed offices and member banks—with encryption protection.

An interesting development occurred a few months after the two-way authentication system was implemented. The Chicago Fed took a call from someone claiming to be a member bank, and wishing to make a multimillion-dollar third-party wire transfer. The Fed operator asked for the next code in sequence, and the caller could not respond. The Fed operator then called back the member bank and inquired about the transfer request, and the bank denied knowledge of it.

Suspicious, the Fed operator reported it to management, who notified the authorities. When tracing the call, it was found that the telephone used to request the wire transfer was a pay phone in the state prison.

There were other attempts to penetrate Fedwire, but these also were unsuccessful. However, these all would have been successful if perpetrated just a few months earlier.

Late 1970s

The Fed began in earnest to automate Fedwire in the middle to late 1970s. Fedwire was upgraded to a "message switching network."

What is a message switching network?

Each wire funds transfer is a "message." As each such "message" is received by the Fed, it is "protected" by making multiple copies of it on magnetic disc and tape, and only then is an acknowledgment sent back to the sender by the Fed. Upon receipt of this acknowledgment, the Fed, in essence, is telling the sender, "We verify that we have your wire instructions, we are debiting your reserve account accordingly; the funds have been sent to the party you specified, and the only way to get them back is to ask the recipient to send them back."

These "messages" then moved, or were "switched," from one Fed District to another through Culpeper.

Let's look briefly at the structure of the network.

Each Federal Reserve bank served as a "hub" in the network, with member banks being directly connected to the Fed Districts' computers through hard-wired terminal connections, or through bank-computer to Fed-computer connections. Thus, there were twelve hubs in the network, one in each Fed District.

In addition, there was a "central hub" in Culpeper, Virginia, to which all 12 Fed Districts interconnected. The routing of a "message" would be from the originating member bank to the originating Fed District , to Culpeper, to the receiving Fed

District, and to receiving member bank. Everything was routed through Culpeper, the "central switch."

There were "redundancies" built into the hardware and software of the entire network to preclude the network from being inoperable because of a malfunction.

For example, Culpeper had four message-switching computers, and each Fed District had two. Culpeper could continue to operate if two of its computers became inoperable, and each Fed District could operate with one.

There were also "recovery" capabilities in the network so that no "message" could be lost or unaccounted for, once the Fed acknowledged receipt—despite whatever hardware or software malfunction or human error occurred.

Bomb Shelter

The Culpeper facility that housed the central switch is in the Federal Reserve Bank of Richmond District.

It is carved into the mountains in Virginia, about 100 miles south of Washington, D.C. The front of the building has large windows, which can be covered with five-foot-thick steel plates in the event of an emergency. These plates are on "rollers" and meet in the center, forming an impenetrable barrier.

In addition to housing the central switch in the 1970s and 1980s, Culpeper was the emergency relocation site for the Fed. It has filtered air handling systems, emergency water and food supplies, an emergency currency supply, communications, and living accommodations for key Fed personnel and their families.

In the event of an emergency, such as the threat of an attack upon the United States, those at the Board designated as key personnel were to make their way to Culpeper with their families, in order to survive and thus to continue the functions of a central bank, should an actual attack occur.

When I was with the Board, there were seven beds in the

facility with my name, and the names of my wife and my children, on them.

The Culpeper facility has since been closed by the Fed.

The "Unknown" of Miller's Move to Treasury

In 1978, President Carter appointed G. William Miller to replace Burns as chairman, and being a businessman, Miller fully understood the importance of, and was a strong advocate of, continued automation of the Fed.

Some writers have been critical of his performance as chairman, for example, one stating he had no interest in monetary policy, and another, that he did a poor job.

With regard to the former, I interfaced with Miller daily. I specifically recall his reaction when he was proposed by President Carter to be Secretary of the Treasury, and Volcker was proposed to replace him as chairman of the Fed.

I had been at Lake Anna with my family, and my brother Ron and his family, on a Friday enjoying the lake—which is about 70 miles directly south of Washington, D.C. On the way home, we stopped at a restaurant to have dinner. While we were eating, the newscaster reported that Miller was being moved to Treasury and that Volcker was replacing him as Fed chairman.

That following Monday, George Mitchell and I had an appointment with Miller in the morning. I said to him, "You really kept this quiet. I was shocked when I heard of it on Friday while having dinner. How long have you known about this?

He said, "Jim, I found out about it the same time you did."

I said, "You mean no one in the White House called to talk to you about it, or to get your reaction—or at least to notify you of this?"

He said, "That's right."

I was shocked by his answer, but not surprised.

During Carter's presidency, the Washington TV news media reported on foulups that occurred in his administration.

For example, one evening a scene was broadcast on the local TV news showing President Carter and an African standing at attention at the White House while the foreigner's national anthem was being played. The commentator said," You know what's wrong with this picture? It's not the national anthem of the person standing next to the president." They had played the wrong national anthem.

On another occasion, the local TV news showed a scene on TV of a U.S. senator standing in the rain. They showed the same scene again with a caption that read, fifteen minutes had elapsed, and then again showed the senator standing in the rain with a caption that noted that twenty-five minutes had elapsed. The commentator then stated that it is "the senator who is critical to getting support for the Carter Administration's key proposal. A White House car was supposed to pick up the senator, and is late, resulting in him standing in the rain for about a half hour."

President Carter has been referred to by some historians as being one of the most intelligent people ever to hold office. But it appeared to me that the people he brought into his administration from Georgia just didn't know how to get things done in Washington and never learned.

One day my secretary, Carol Slocumbe, came into my office and said, "The Executive Office of the President is on the phone." Of course I immediately picked up the phone and on the line was a man who identified himself as an assistant to the president. He briefly discussed President Carter's plan to reorganize the way the Federal government does business. (This was publicized as a major initiative during Carter's Administration, and given the same level of attention as the Cap and Trade and Health Reform proposals today.) The man on the phone asked me to come to the Executive Office Building to meet with him and some others. The Executive Office Building stands just to the right and in front of the White House as you look south from Pennsylvania Avenue.

I went to the room he mentioned and met a young man from Georgia and a professor from MIT. They asked me to be a member of a team they were assembling to review and make recommendations to the president on how the Federal government acquires computers. The MIT professor was to be the chairman of the group, which was to complete its review within six months.

I asked the young man what would be done with the results of our review. He stated, "The group will prepare a two-page memorandum summarizing its recommendations for the president's review, and he will check off those that he wants implemented." I asked how much the government spends annually on computers and was told, "About $4 billion."

I declined the invitation—but as I did, I wondered why the president would personally pay attention to how the government acquires computers in view of all the pressing issues requiring his attention.

The Miller Rumors and Pedestrian Analysis

That Monday morning, when meeting with Miller, I asked him what he intended to do in view of his announced shift to the Treasury. He stated that his preference would be to remain as Fed chairman, but "if the President asks you to do something, you do it."

I was disappointed to learn that Miller would be leaving the Fed. He was the first accomplished and successful business manager ever appointed as Fed chairman, and 83 percent of the job required such a background.

As previously mentioned, some writers have given him a poor grade in assessing his performance as Fed chairman. Woodward, in his book, *Maestro,* stated that Greenspan felt that Miller was weak and ineffective by allowing the FOMC to vote as they wanted without much guidance or influence from him. It is unclear as to whether Greenspan told this to Woodward, or if others did. In any event, it is highly unusual for one Fed chairman to criticize another.

Martin in his book, *Greenspan, the Man Behind Money,* states that Miller was a disaster.

Jones, in his book, *Unlocking the Secrets of the Fed,* states that Miller amazingly seemed uninterested in macroeconomic policy, and earned, by consensus, a failing grade as Fed chairman.

These three authors are repeating what has been told to them by others. In graduate school, we referred to this as "pedestrian analysis." They did not know Miller, nor did they work with him daily, as I did.

The first two of these authors are professional writers and relied upon interviews for their material.

Jones is just flat-out wrong about Miller's disinterest in monetary policy, and his comment about Miller earning a failing grade by consensus is based upon his "rating system" which left much to be desired.

Let me set the record straight.

G. William Miller was Fed chairman for seventeen months, during 1978 and 1979. Economists readily admit that it takes as much as 2.5 years before Fed actions on monetary policy work their way through the economy and can "be felt." Eventually, what the Fed did with monetary policy, while Miller was chairman, wasn't "felt" in the economy until Volcker replaced him. Moreover, what was "felt" while Miller was Fed chairman were the actions of his predecessor, Arthur Burns.

Now let's look briefly at the resources and people behind monetary policy upon which all Fed chairmen rely.

While Miller was chairman, the "second most powerful person on the FOMC" was Paul Volcker, who was then the president of the New York Fed. Did Volcker "fall asleep" as FOMC vice chairman while Miller supposedly misdirected monetary policy? Or did he abdicate his responsibilities? I doubt it.

The composition of the FOMC was essentially the same when Miller was Fed chairman as it was when Volcker replaced him—with one exception. There was a new president of the New York Fed. Did the FOMC suddenly become uninformed when Miller was Fed chairman and miscast their votes? I doubt that also.

The key staff person for monetary policy at the Board when Miller was chairman, was Steve Axilrod, referred to by some in the press as "little Napoleon" because of his strong influence. He was also there when Volcker was chairman, and when Burns was chairman before Miller. Moreover, most of the monetary-policy staff was common to all three chairmen. Did they suddenly lose touch with what was going on in the economy and give bad advice to Miller and the FOMC for seventeen months? I don't think so.

The Fed had come a long way in its wire and securities-transfer capabilities from the operations in place when Burns became chairman. Security was improved a thousandfold. The Board in Washington was the controlling factor in the development of the message-switching capabilities in Fedwire and its approval was required for everything that was upgraded in the network.

Virtually all decisions were made as a result of work done in the pyramid structure (discussed earlier). Board staff members were very much involved in task forces, subcommittees, and committees of the conferences, where much detailed, hands-on planning and execution took place. In those days, we lived out of a suitcase.

In this regard, one day I received a call in my office from John Kakalec, who was the controller of the Board. Arthur Burns was then chairman, and no doubt he had instructed the Board's controller to carefully review all expenditures. I know this, because he continually reminded me, and the entire Board and its staff, that we were "custodians of the public purse."

Each year the Fed turns over to the Treasury its earnings after it deducts all of its operating costs, and these earnings are significant. The majority of such earnings come from the huge portfolio of government securities that the Fed manipulates in conducting monetary policy, but some earnings do come from fees that the Fed charges financial institutions and the U.S. Treasury for services, and from profits (or losses) on foreign exchange transactions.

The last year I was at the Board, in 1981, the Fed turned over $14 billion to the U.S. Treasury. At the end of 2005, the Fed gave the Treasury $21.5 billion. The largest amount transferred by the Fed to Treasury was $27 billion in 2001. Burns strongly believed that it was our job to maximize this amount by being careful and prudent in how we spent the public's money.

I got on the phone with John Kakalec and he told me that he was having problems with one of my staff members and wanted me to talk to him.

He proceeded to tell me that Brian Carey had submitted an expense account for his most recent travel, and included the cost of a hat, which he lost on the trip. John sent the expense form back to Brian, denying payment, and telling him to remove the hat and that then it would be approved.

Brian returned the expense payment form to John, and the lost hat was not listed as an expense. I said to John, "Well, what's the problem?" He said, "The total amount requested by Brian hasn't changed, and there was a little note on his resubmitted request that said: "The hat's still in there, find it if you can.""

I told John to pay Brian and again reminded him that travel was not a benefit. (John had told me previously that our staff should consider travel as a privilege.) Of course, John hardly ever traveled on Fed business and remained entrenched comfortably in Washington.

Since I was a division director, I was entitled to fly first-class. So were the Board members. During the Board's budget preparation the following year, the Board's staff director for administration, John Denkler, a retired Navy captain whom I assisted in joining the Board's staff, came to my office for a visit. (I had worked for John when I was in the Navy, and he was a colleague of mine in graduate school.) He told me that he had been reviewing travel expenses with Chairman Burns and said that Burns told him to inform me that he (Burns) always flies coach class. The object of his visit was to get me to reduce my travel costs. I told John that I was away from my office 60–70 percent of the time, and that I will continue to fly first-class until the Board policy is changed. I also told him that when Burns flies coach, he is recognized as a VIP and given first-class treatment. That would not happen to me.

Burns never ceased to be cognizant of the "custodian of the public purse" concept. A few of the Board members told me that Burns tried the same approach on them—and they also refused to downgrade their flying arrangements.

This is the only time I can recall anyone in the Fed not following Burns's lead.

I am reminded of another incident that involved Brian. We both were on the West Coast, meeting with Marshall Data Communications, whose message-switching computers were used in Fedwire. In the evening, one of their owners, Ken Morioka, took us out to a very nice restaurant for dinner.

On the menu was listed a 125-year-old brandy for $125 an ounce. After dinner, our host asked us if we would like to try it. I declined, being a beer and wine drinker, but Brian and Ken ordered it.

The waiter and the head waiter made a big show out of bringing the brandy to the table in a small "vault." They unlocked the vault, took out the bottle, and very carefully poured two one-ounce glasses. By this time, the attention of the entire restaurant was riveted on our table. It was not a common occurrence at this restaurant for anyone to order a $125 one-ounce glass of brandy, let alone two.

They carefully positioned the glasses on the table in front of our host and Brian, and Brian said to them, "You got any coke to go with this?" The head waiter was so taken aback, he was caught off guard and couldn't respond. The place erupted in laughter.

Walter Wriston

In order to establish and promote communication between the Fed and commercial banks nationwide, the Federal Reserve Act provided for a Federal Advisory Council. This council consists of twelve people, one from each of the twelve Fed districts, who are appointed to the council to serve for one year by the Boards of Directors of the twelve Fed banks. This council meets with the Board of Governors in Washington, and with Board staff, once each quarter.

Walter Wriston, at that time chairman of Citibank, was on the council, representing the Second Fed District, when I met with him at one of these quarterly meetings in the mid-1970s. (Council members inform the Board's secretary about whom they wish to meet with, and schedules are arranged.)

I met with him and a few other council members in the Board's Special Library. Wriston, and one of his executive officers at Citibank, John Reed, were interested in getting the Fed to extend the closing hour of Fedwire. I told him that sounded like a reasonable request, and that I would pursue it.

The very next quarter, I again met with Wriston—and he gave me accolades, stating that was the fastest he had seen the Fed move on anything; he stated this because the Fedwire closing hour was extended during that quarter and prior to his second meeting with me.

I thanked him, and walked out of the Special Library. Here was one of the biggest names in banking at the time, appreciative of what the Fed had done for him.

But there was something I didn't tell him at our first meeting. We in the Fed had already decided to extend the closing hour of Fedwire, and so it was a done deal. Only no one outside the Fed was aware of it.

This was one time, perhaps the only time, that the major bankers in our nation applauded the speed with which the Fed was able to get something done. I had heard enough complaints from them—and thought it was time we turned the table.

1980s

The Fed started planning for the replacements for the message-switching network in the late 1970s.

Brian Carey was hired by the Fed as project manager. He left the Board staff and moved to the Chicago Fed, where the project was based. He hired a staff, and began working with the primary vendor, Northern Telecom, a Canadian firm, to develop and implement a "package-switching network."

I was on the committee overseeing the project. Dan Doyle, first vice president of the Chicago Fed was on it, and others. I left the Fed in 1981 before the project was completed.

What is a package-switching network?

It is a network that is capable of moving "packets" of information nationally throughout the Federal Reserve System. The network is constructed so that each Federal Reserve Bank has multiple paths to all other Federal Reserve Banks.

The information to be moved on the network is placed into "packets." The number of packets is dependent upon the volume of information to be moved.

Each "packet" contains header and control information and each packet is routed to its destination point—independently from all other packets—in an expedited manner utilizing the first available circuitry.

At the destination point, the packets are reassembled into the proper sequence, and the information is removed from the packets and delivered.

Let's assume the New York Fed wishes to send information to the San Francisco Fed that requires three packets to contain it. The first packet may be delivered to the San Francisco Fed via the Chicago and the Kansas City Feds because their circuitry to San Francisco is "open." The second packet may be delivered via the Philadelphia and Atlanta Feds for the same reason. The third packet may be delivered via the Richmond and Dallas Feds.

The packets are reassembled into the proper sequence after they are received by the San Francisco Fed. For example, packet three may have arrived first in San Francisco; packet two, second; and packet one, last. The sequence of arrivals of the packets depends upon what else is being transmitted on the network concurrently with these three packets, and the priority of such. The packets are removed and the information is delivered to the recipient at the San Francisco Fed.

The packet-switching network handled all of the Fed's communications requirements, including wire transfers, securities transfers, research data, etc., until the early 1990s.

All Federal Reserve banks, branches, offices, and the Board were interconnected. Member banks and other financial institutions and organizations inputted and received their wire funds transfers and government securities transfers via terminal and computer links to the Federal Reserve bank or branch servicing them. The network, of course, was used to move these wires and securities transfers between Fed Districts.

The network had encryption protection. The day it was turned on, it worked. That gives you an indication of the thoroughness of planning for it. (That is one thing the Fed has consistently excelled at over the years—thorough and successful planning.)

Fedwire Today

Fedwire today is run out of one of the Fed's three main-frame computer centers that are located in New York (East Rutherford, New Jersey), Dallas, and Richmond. (The Fed prefers that the actual location not be disclosed.) Technological advancements, including greatly expanded bandwidths enabling large volume and rapid data communications, have made it possible to interconnect all Fed offices, and their constituency, into one mainframe in a remote location for the purpose of effecting wire funds and security transfers.

Under older technology including "message switching" and "packet switching," each Fed bank had its own computer facility supporting Fedwire. This is no longer necessary.

Fedwire also includes mainframe redundancy with a "hot" backup site, and a "warm" backup site in the event of failure of the prime site for whatever reason. The switch to a backup site is done periodically to ensure the viability of the concept—and it actually has been employed in one situation.

Today, there are a total of about 9,500 financial institutions, government organizations, and other users interconnected to Fedwire, and about 8,200 have "online" connections, including about 350 with computer links. Of these, 120 users account for 80 percent of the 126 million wire transfers carried out each year, and 50 users account for 80 percent of the dollars moved on Fedwire. Over $2.1 trillion is moved on Fedwire each business day.

The users' fees for Fedwire range from cents per wire transfer for "online" input, to $15 or more per transfer for "offline" input (e.g., a telephone input of wire transfer instructions). Considering the service provided, this is easily the finest banking service for the least cost on the planet.

The Fed—as owner and operator of the world's money-moving and settlement system—greatly improved the security and operational capability of Fedwire. George Mitchell initiated and headed the effort as chairman of the Board's Committee on the Payments Mechanism during Burns's tenure, and the effort continued when Miller, Volcker, and then Greenspan respectfully, became chairmen.

Automated Clearing House (ACH)

The ACH is a nationwide automated payment system that Mitchell was instrumental in initiating in the early to middle 1970s. The development of the ACH was a cooperative arrangement between the Fed and commercial bankers. Today, ten billion payments are cleared and settled through ACH facilities each year. The banking cost to process an ACH item is about 1 mil, according to Elliott McEntee, president of the National

97

Automated Clearing House Association, which compares favorably with the banking cost for a check of about eight cents.

Whereas the average size of a payment on Fedwire was $3.9 million, the average size of a payment made through the Automated Clearing House was and is very substantially smaller. Differing technological capabilities are required for each type of payment. You don't need instantaneous movement of "good funds" for the smaller payments handled through the ACH, as you do in Fedwire. Therefore, you don't build a Mercedes if a Volkswagen will do.

The ACH is designed to handle small-dollar-value, repetitive-type payments in an automated manner. Monthly mortgage payments, electric bills, gas bills, water bills, and social security payments are examples of the type of payments efficiently handled through the ACH.

When ACH operations began in our nation in the late 1970s, these repetitive payments were recorded on to magnetic tape in a prescribed format, and the financial institutions participating in the ACH accepted such magnetic images for the payment or receipt of funds attendant with the details on the tape. In essence, the tape contained the same detailed information as a check, but since the information was in magnetic form—rather than on paper—it was more efficient and less costly to process.

Each item on tape contained: a payee, (your name, for example); a payor (your electric company); the payee's bank and account number (your bank account, from which funds are to be taken to pay the electric bill); the payor's bank and account number (your electric company's account, into which funds are to be placed); the dollar amount; and the date on which payment is to be made.

Repetitive-type payments can be handled efficiently in the ACH since the only data that change each month are the dollar amount and the date of payment. All other items on the tape had to be inputted just once, and then were generated automatically each month.

In the intervening years since start-up of the ACH, technology has been used to refine the system, and magnetic tape as a means of payment exchange has been replaced by more sophisticated communications technologies. Most ACH transactions are now exchanged among participating financial institutions via data links.

The settlement for ACH transactions occurs on Fed books—through member banks' reserve accounts and through the clearing accounts maintained with the Fed by other financial institutions.

The Fed's participation in the ACH at the outset was as the processor of the information on magnetic tape, as well as providing settlement capabilities. Today, the Fed is still the largest processor, with over 50 percent of the items cleared and settled through one of the Fed's three computer centers used to process ACH items. In 2005, of the total of 14 billion ACH payments in the nation, the Fed processed 7.4 billion of these with a value of $16 trillion. The remaining 6.6 billion of ACH payments are processed in private clearing arrangements and settled through the Fed. Virtually all financial institutions participating in the ACH are members of the National Automated Clearing House Association (NACHA). I can recall some interesting meetings that we in the Fed had with commercial bankers as the ACH was being developed.

In the mid-1970s, I was part of a Fed committee that met with representatives of the American Bankers Association (ABA) to review and discuss Fed regulations pertaining to ACH payments, among other operational matters. The ABA group consisted of commercial bankers that were representing the banking industry in the development of the ACH.

On one occasion, we met in a conference room at the Watergate Hotel in Washington. The "setting" of the room is important to what took place, so let me describe it to you. I was sitting at a conference table situated in the middle of the room with eleven others—five Fed people and six commercial bankers. In addition, there were about ten to fifteen other commercial bankers sitting in chairs around the conference table.

I was in the process of responding to one of the questions

that a banker had asked, after we had told them that we couldn't do what they desired, and I had just said, "I am sympathetic to your position," when another banker, sitting in a chair around the table, interrupted me and said, "Sympathy is a word between syphilis and shit in the dictionary; don't give us that crap." Of course, the whole room erupted in laughter.

I looked at the banker, an older man with gray hair, from one of the banks in Kansas City and obviously not an introvert. I must admit that my first thought was to stand up, announce that the meeting had ended, and walk out the door. A microsecond later, I thought, "Don't get mad, get even."

The laughter in the room eventually subsided, and all eyes made there way back to me, sitting at the table.

I again looked at the banker from Kansas City, and said very calmly, "Since you are so proficient in the placement of words in the dictionary, perhaps you can tell us where 'asshole' is found."

Laughter again exploded in the room. And that banker never said another word during the remainder of the meeting.

This meeting was an exception. Although anger and impatience would surface from time to time among the Fed people and bankers attending these meetings, we would generally avoid this kind of "crustiness."

I recall another incident related to ACH developments that occurred at about the same time at the Treasury.

Les Plumly, the man who is responsible for the direct deposit of Social Security benefits, which is now a nationwide program, invited the commercial bankers and other financial people to the U.S. Treasury Building for a meeting. At this meeting, he unveiled the plan to make Social Security payments directly to a recipient's account with a financial institution through the ACH.

After he finished his briefing, a banker, very well dressed in a three-piece, pin striped suit and an expensive tie, raised his hand, and was recognized by Les.

The banker said, "This is all fine and good. But what are

you going to pay us to receive Social Security payments in this manner?"

Les looked at the banker and said, "I'm going to be giving you a deposit in your bank each and every month, and you want me to pay you? Where did you go to school? What's wrong with you?"

At about that time, the banker realized he was not only on thin ice, he was sunk. No other bankers came to his defense. Instead, they lowered their eyes in embarrassment.

Sometimes the best-dressed guy isn't the smartest.

European Developments

While ACH start-up developments were going on in our country, the Europeans had already implemented automated payment systems that performed similar functions. Thus, we had an opportunity to benefit from their experience.

Fed representatives, including Mitchell and I, made a number of trips to Europe to review their automated payment systems. Invariably, such trips would either start or end in Basel, home of the BIS.

It was both of concern to me and educational to learn that as far back as the early to middle 1970s, European countries were having to take precautions against terrorists.

The very first time I landed at the Basel airport, I noticed a large number of military personnel with automated weapons patrolling inside and outside of the terminal. When I asked Kevin Kearney what was going on, he stated, "Terrorist precautions."

Likewise, when touring the BIS's new building for the first time, I was surprised by the number of anti-terrorist protections that were designed into the building, such as special glass windows that could withstand the firing power of large caliber weapons.

We also visited the Bundesbank, Germany's central bank, in Frankfurt. We stayed at the "homestead," a facility for housing the Bundesbank's guests that is located on bank property. The Bundesbank was enclosed by a wire fence, with barbed wire on top of the fence.

The first morning there, I had awakened early and went out to jog. It was still dark. As soon as I stepped outside the homestead, I ran into a military guard who had an automated weapon and a large German shepherd on a leash. I then noticed that the perimeter of the bank's property was being constantly patrolled by many armed guards with dogs. It looked like a scene from a James Bond movie.

Inquiring that morning as to the reason for such guards, I was told by Rolf Engler that there had been terrorist attacks made on the bank.

At the time, that seemed so foreign and far away.

The Bundesbank has the world's largest collection of ancient gold coins, dating back to Caesar's time and beyond. It takes about a half day to review all of these, and it is well worth the time.

The bank owns a large number of private residences (we would call them apartments) and employees of the bank are housed in these. This is considered part of their compensation. Housing in Germany was and is very expensive.

I recall having a BIS group visit my home in Virginia, and Rolf Engler was among these. As he stood in the entryway of my home he said, "I am amazed that you could own a home like this." He was, perhaps, 20 years older than me and getting close to retirement. He said he could never own a house like that in Germany. That surprised me, because Rolf was at the same level in the Bundesbank that I was at the Fed. As I later learned, housing construction in Germany at the time did not make use of the technological advancements of our country. In essence each new construction was a unique "hand-built" home in Germany, and they were very expensive.

We always enjoyed our visits to the BIS.

The professional staff had access to a tennis club funded by the BIS that had numerous clay courts, all well maintained, and food was unbelievably inexpensive at the club by Basel standards. Obviously, it was heavily subsidized.

We had an opportunity, in the mid-1970s, to do some consulting on payment system matters for the BIS when I was with the Fed. Elliott McEntee, now the CEO of NACHA, and I were given what we thought was an unusually large amount of per diem in Swiss Francs (the equivalent of $3,000) to cover our out-of-pocket expenses for a week. As it turned out, we needed it. We took Kevin Kearney and his wife, Shirley, out for pizza and beer while we were there. For four of us, the bill was equivalent to $400—that's for pizza and beer.

We played tennis at their club every morning before we started work and in the evening as well. Kevin had a very attractive Frenchwoman on his staff, Jacqueline, who was the fourth in our doubles play. It was Kevin and I versus McEntee and Jacqueline. The problem was that Jacqueline had a boyfriend, a British fellow who did not look kindly on our spending so much time with her. He kept his distance while we were on the court, but nonetheless observed most of our games. He also chastised McEntee for "being loud" on the court. (McEntee was about his age.) I think what really set him off was our applauding when a ball went over the waist-high fence on the left side of the court, and Jacqueline reached over the fence to get it, exposing her panties beneath her tennis skirt.

The two best meals I ever had were as a guest of the BIS in the late 1970s.

One was as Schleiminger's guest for lunch. Schleiminger hosted Mitchell, Kevin, and me. He took us to what once was a castle in Basel, but had been converted to a restaurant because it became too expensive to retain as a residence. We had "unborn lamb," white asparagus (it's harvested before it comes out of the ground), oven-baked potatoes, fresh strawberries, and a rare wine (according to Kevin).

The other was as a guest of the central bank of Belgium, a member of the BIS. Our host took us to The Swan, the public portion of which is a five-star restaurant in the central square in Brussels. Directly above the restaurant is a "private club" operated by the same management, where we ate.

Nine of us had dinner: Mitchell and his wife, Mary; Jim Mcintosh, first vice president of the Boston Fed, and his wife, Liz; me and my wife, Ginny; our host and his wife, and another person from the central bank of Belgium whose wife could not attend.

Our host asked us if we would mind if he did the ordering for everyone and of course, we all agreed. The entire meal was indeed the best I ever had, including the lobster bisque, lamb chops, and wine.

I mentioned those who attended this dinner for three reasons.

First, we had eight waiters assigned to our table for the entire evening, serving nine of us.

Second, I was able to see the bill and it came to the equivalent of $270.00 per person, the most expensive meal I ever had. Today, that meal would cost $922.34 per person after adjusting for inflation during the intervening years.

Third, our host was able to effortlessly keep all participants involved in the dinner conversation, including wives—for four hours.

During that same trip we had gone to Paris to meet with a representative of the Bank of France, the country's central bank. He had arranged to have a bank car and driver take our wives sightseeing for the entire day. We, in turn—Mitchell, Mcintosh, and I—met with him for eleven hours, discussing payments mechanism matters. He had an interpreter at the meeting. When he spoke French, it would be interpreted for us in English. When we spoke English, it would be interpreted for him in French. Thus the reason for the eleven-hour meeting.

Afterward, on our way out of the bank, Mitchell said, "Can you believe that? And I know that son of a bitch speaks English as well as we do."

We moved on to Basel, Switzerland, to meet with the Bank for International Settlements (BIS). Mitchell, Mcintosh, myself, and our wives checked into the Kraft Hotel—which is a boutique type of hotel right on the Rhine River with about 50 guest rooms. As my wife and I were getting settled in our room, the phone rang and when I picked it up, Mcintosh was on the other end. He said, "How is your room?"

I answered, "Fine. We have a nice large room with two groupings of double French doors leading to a patio overlooking the Rhine."

He responded, "Why don't you and Ginny come to our room and have a look."

He gave me their room number, which was on a lower floor, and we proceeded down the stairs to that number. I knocked on the door, he opened it, and we stepped into a room that was barely larger than the twin bed it had in it. The hotel had put Jim and Liz into the last room available, and expected them to share that twin bed. We all laughed, and they checked out of the hotel and moved to the Hilton, which was closer to the BIS.

6

All About Money

Most everyone uses currency and coins daily in this country. It is the most common method of making payments in our nation. The American Bankers Association reported in its July 2003 study that cash is used to pay 32 percent of all purchases made at the point of sale. (Debit cards are used 31 percent of the time; credit cards, 21 percent; checks, 15 percent; and prepaid cards [gift cards], 2 percent of the time.)

There are alternatives available to the use of currency and coins, including checks, debit and credit cards, and other electronic payment means, and the use of these account for a substantial amount of our financial transactions. Because of the technology infrastructure that has been developed, which makes widespread use of electronic payments possible, more and more cash transactions are being displaced.

Banking industry visionaries, such as former vice chairman George Mitchell, looked into the future and saw a society that could function without currency and coins. It is far less costly to society to use electronic payment systems—which you access with your debit or credit card—than it is to use currency and coins to make your financial transactions.

But we still use currency and coins extensively in our society—and may not ever totally displace their use with electronic means of making payments.

So let's look behind the scenes and see what it takes to keep currency and coin available as a means of value exchange.

Composition of Money

Approximately 5 percent of the total value of money in circulation is in the form of coins, and 95 percent is in the form of paper money, our currency. About $35 billion worth of coins is in circulation, and $794 billion in currency. Of this latter amount about 80 percent is in $50 and $100 notes.

About 1.2 percent of the value of currency in circulation is in $1 notes; .2 percent is in $2 notes; 1.4 percent is in $5 notes; 2.2 percent is in $10 notes; 15.6 percent is in $20 notes; 8.7 percent is in $50 notes; and 70.6 percent is in $100 notes.

Of the total number of notes in circulation, 26 percent are $50 and $100 notes, 30 percent are $10 and $20 notes, and 44 percent are $1, $2, and $5 notes.

Federal Reserve Note

Each of the above referenced denominations of our currency cited above has the words "Federal Reserve Note" imprinted on it. Why, and what does this mean?

About 99 percent of the $794 billion in circulation is in the form of Federal Reserve Notes. The remaining 1 percent is in the form of U.S. notes, National Bank Notes, and silver certificates, which are still legal currency.

Until 1914, our currency consisted of notes issued primarily by the U.S. Treasury, which were secured by gold or silver. These forms of currency were so limited in amount that additional currency could not easily be supplied when it was needed in the economy.

Under the Federal Reserve Act, the Federal Reserve System was charged with making available a currency that responds to the needs of the nation.

When currency is needed, the Fed will supply Federal Reserve Notes to member banks and other financial institutions and charge their reserve account or clearing balance for the dollar amount of the currency issued. These financial institutions, in turn, will supply their customers with the currency they require—and charge their accounts accordingly.

The customers of these financial institutions, particularly businesses, will make deposits of currency resulting from cash sales that are made. When such deposits exceed the currency requirements of the financial institution, they will return the excess Federal Reserve Notes to the Fed and their reserve account or clearing balance will be credited with the dollar amount of the currency returned.

In 2005, the Fed banks received 37.2 billion Federal Reserve Notes, worth $639 billion, sent to them by financial institutions, and supplied to them 38.5 billion notes worth about $677 billion to meet their currency needs.

Of the 19,000 commercial banks, savings and loans, mutual savings banks, and credit unions operating in our nation, 10,300 deal directly with the Fed to meet their currency requirements. The others rely upon those of the 10,300 that provide correspondent services to the remaining 8,700.

Whereas gold and silver previously backed our nation's currency, it is now, in essence, backed by the reserves that member banks are required to maintain with the Fed, and ultimately, by the full faith and credit of the U.S. Government.

Printing of Currency

The Treasury, the Bureau of Engraving and Printing (BEP), and the Fed all get involved in the printing of our currency.

The Treasury and the Fed jointly determine the denominations of notes to be printed, and also, make the decisions on any redesigns of our currency that occur from time to time.

The BEP offices in Washington, D.C., and Fort Worth, Texas, print the notes. Currency is printed on special paper, which includes features difficult to replicate. Sheets of thirty-two notes are printed concurrently. These are then cut into individual notes. Each note is imprinted with a unique serial number.

Cost

When I left the Fed in 1981, the cost of printing 1,000 Federal Reserve Notes was $17. The weighted average cost rose to $56 per 1,000 notes in 2005, and it has since risen somewhat. The least expensive notes to print at that time were the $1 and $2 denominations, which cost $42.97 per 1,000 notes. The $5 denomination cost $57.27 per 1,000; tens, twenties, and fifties cost $80.58 per 1,000 and 100s cost $70.10 per 1,000.

About half of the cost increase between 1981 and the present for printing notes is due to inflation, and the remainder to the enhanced security features included in the notes.

The Fed determines how much of each denomination to print and instructs the BEP accordingly.

Distribution

An armored vehicle is used for ground transportation of currency. Commercial flights are used for air transportation. The larger-denomination notes are transported by air, and the smaller notes by ground. The Fed budgeted $16.3 million for currency transportation in 2006, of which $12.5 million was for new currency shipments from the BEP to Fed banks, and $3.8 million for currency shipments among Fed banks. These numbers have increased since that time. The latter move currency from Fed Banks with excess fit currency to those that would otherwise require new currency shipments from the BEP.

Thus, currency is distributed from the BEP to each Fed bank and branch. Member banks and other depository institutions then order deliveries of currency from Reserve banks and branches, as required, to meet their customers' demands.

You probably have been on some commercial flights that were "hauling" currency on behalf of the Fed and you didn't realize it. Next time, pay attention to the loading of baggage and you might spot it.

The armored vehicle is driven to the baggage loading area.

The currency is the last item loaded on the plane. The courier observes the loading and does not leave the area until the baggage compartment is locked and secured. The courier is the last one to board the plane and the first one off to observe the unloading of the currency.

Attempted Theft

In the mid 1960s, an attempt made to steal currency that was being transported on a commercial flight is noteworthy.

The perpetrator was able to make his way from the passenger cabin to the baggage hold while the flight was in progress. He removed panels in the bathroom and then replaced them as he lowered himself into the luggage hold. The stewardess found the bathroom locked, and since no one responded to her calls, the bathroom was opened and found empty. It was an unusual occurrence, and it was assumed that the latch locking the door somehow had engaged during the flight.

The flight landed at its destination, and while taxiing to the gate, the pilot noticed that the light became illuminated, indicating an open luggage door. He assumed an electrical failure.

The courier was the first person off of the plane and saw that, indeed, the luggage door was open. Peeking inside, he noticed movement in the packages containing the currency being transported, so he alerted the authorities.

The perpetrator was apprehended while climbing over the fence, attempting to leave airport property with new, previously uncirculated, Federal Reserve Notes.

Since the serial numbers of these notes had been recorded, even if the perpetrator were successful, it would have been difficult to circulate these notes without drawing considerable attention.

Removing the Unfit Notes

When member banks, and other financial depository institutions return notes to the Fed, these are checked so that unfit notes can be removed from circulation. The process of returning notes involves scheduling an armored vehicle pick-up so that the notes can be safely transported to the local Fed office.

Prior to the early 1980s, the process of outsorting unfit notes and counterfeit notes was done manually. When you walked into the Fed area where this was done, you observed a group of women, each woman operating under a light with a rubber sleeve on her thumb, sorting through stacks of currency, one note at a time. The unfit notes would be placed in a discard stack, and the counterfeit notes in another. The usable currency would be placed in a third stack and returned to circulation.

And there were observers in the room who did nothing but watch the Fed's employees engaging in the process. They were part of the dual-control security system. This prevented one person alone from acting dishonestly. It would take two or more persons to successfully perpetrate a theft in this process.

The first time I saw this operation, I wondered how many counterfeit notes made it through this process, because these women were shuffling those notes at a remarkably high rate of speed. Unfit notes, on the other hand, were easier to spot.

In the late 1970s, the Fed initiated a project to automate the process by constructing a machine that would outsort the fit notes from the unfit and counterfeit notes.

The project was completed via the pyramid structure described earlier.

Technologies from all over the world were combined, and eventually, in the early to middle 1980s, a machine was constructed that successfully could accomplish the task.

For example, the currency transport mechanism that was required was found in Germany. (The Fed had to have a transport mechanism that could select and move one note at a time from a stack of notes that contained crisp new notes as well as

111

soft, old, crumpled notes, and everything in between—without jamming. And this had to be done at a very high rate of speed.)

Many of the design changes that have occurred in our currency have facilitated the automated outsorting of unfit and counterfeit currency, in addition to making counterfeiting more difficult.

How many unfit notes are outsorted each year?

A total of 6.6 billion unfit notes were outsorted and destroyed in 2005, with a value of $83.2 billion. The cost to manufacture replacements for those notes was $479 million. These numbers have since increased.

The Fed Bank of Atlanta came up with a unique and creative system in the 1970s to motivate the women who were outsorting unfit and counterfeit currency.

The problem that they faced was one of keeping these women motivated because that is all they did—all day.

The Atlanta Fed determined the number of notes a person should reasonably be able to manually sort through in an eight-hour shift. The women were told that after they had sorted through that number of notes, they could go home, and that they would be paid for the full eight hours.

The Atlanta Fed actually increased productivity in this area with the change, and the women were leaving the bank one to two hours earlier than before.

Destruction of Notes

The Fed uses dual controls throughout the note destruction process—meaning two people are involved in each step. As mentioned earlier, this makes it difficult for one person to perpetrate a theft by himself or herself.

Prior to the early 1980s, the first step in the destruction process was counting of the notes to be destroyed. The second step involved punching three large holes in the notes: a rectangle, a circle, and a triangle. The third step involved recounting the notes. (The second count verified the first and was a security feature.) And the fourth step was the incineration of the notes.

Since the automating of the outsorting process, the unfit notes go directly from the machine to a shredder.

In the late 1970s, when the Fed began to test the feasibility of shredding unfit currency, a man made an appointment with my secretary to see me about the shredding process. When I subsequently met with him, he told me that his small firm had successfully made sucrose out of the shredded currency. They were able to extract the ink and other chemicals from the shredded currency, and then used what remained to chemically alter the composition of the material to sucrose. He brought along samples of the finished product with him, and I tasted it (after he did). It did taste like sugar.

The problem, however, was that the cost of this process exceeded the price of sugar off the grocery shelf. He wanted to know if the Fed would be interested in funding continued research in an attempt to lower the processing cost to a level where the end product would be competitive in price to sugar. Then, presumably, rather than discarding the shredded material, we could produce sugar with it.

I politely declined, and told him that such an effort by the Fed would not be consistent with its roles as defined in the Federal Reserve Act.

Inside Job

Despite the dual controls that were used by the Fed in the note destruction process, partially destroyed notes began to appear in the economy of the area served by the Philadelphia Fed in the 1960s. Notes began to show up that contained the three holes—the rectangle, circle, and triangle. Since more than one half of the notes were still there, they were accepted in the economy. (If you have 51 percent of any note, you can take it to the Fed and get a new note for it.)

An investigation discovered that there was collusion going on in the destruction process at the Philadelphia Fed, and some of the partially destroyed notes had been stolen. They were being used in the economy, and that ultimately led to the apprehension of the perpetrators.

Life of Notes

The note with the shortest life span is the $5 note. It lasts 1.25 years before it needs to be replaced. The $1 note has a life span of 21.3 months; the $10 note lasts for 18.3 months; the $20 note, for 24.3 months; the $50 note, for 55.4 months; and the $100 note, for 88.8 months.

Many billions of dollars in currency have remained in circulation beyond expected life spans. This is because some people prefer to hold their savings in our currency rather than in their own country's currency, or in a bank in their own country.

People in countries with high rates of inflation find it more profitable to hold dollars, because inflation and revaluation of their currency diminish their savings, even when considering the high rates of interest they have access to in such countries.

The Fed is not concerned about the amount of such currency that remains outstanding. This dollar amount, in essence, is a free loan to our country. The Fed reported that $794 billion in currency value was outstanding at the end of 2005, and that about two-thirds of this value was held abroad. From 1993 to 2005, the value of currency in circulation increased by 117 percent, much of it ending up in other countries.

The Fed distributes a large amount of currency abroad through "extended custodial inventory facilities" and through select depository institutions. The Fed began doing this in 1996 to facilitate distribution and acceptance of our newly designed currency in foreign markets.

Not on My Watch

There are collectors of currency, like there are of coin and stamps, and other items. While in my office one day in the late 1970s, my secretary informed me that someone from the Treasury Department was on the phone. I picked up the phone and the person identified himself as an assistant to William Simon, who was then Secretary of the Treasury.

The Fed and Treasury were about to issue a new $2 note—for about the eleventh time, as the past issuances had been unsuccessful, and as it turned out, so was this one. I suppose people don't like it because it can be confused with a $1 note. In any event, they don't use it, except at racetracks and in Las Vegas.

The person on the phone said that Secretary Simon was a collector and would like some low-serial-numbered $2 notes, preferably a full sheet, if possible.

I said, "So would I." There was silence on the line.

I told the person, "If Secretary Simon actually wants low-serial-numbered $2 notes that have not been distributed, tell him to submit his name to the lottery drawing that is done for such purposes. If he's lucky, he might get them."

The person responded, "No, you don't understand. Secretary of the Treasury Simon wants the notes."

I responded, "Yes, I do understand. And the lottery is his only chance." After about ten more minutes of discussion, he determined that I was not going to arrange what he desired, so he said, "Well, okay, it looks like we will have to contact Chairman Burns, directly."

I said, "Do you want me to have you connected?"

He said, "No, we know his number," and he hung up.

Afterward, I wondered why the assistant did not go with that request directly to the Bureau of Engraving and Printing, which is under the Treasury Department organizationally. Perhaps it would look better if approval came from the Fed rather than internally. In any event, I never heard another word about it. But if anyone had contacted Burns with such a request, his answer would have been the same as mine.

Smelly Money

During Burns's tenure as chairman, one of the Board members, Jack Sheehan, suggested placing "used" currency in Culpeper as the emergency currency supply.

The rationale for this was that if the country were attacked, the quality of currency in circulation would not be a major consideration. There would be far more pressing matters to deal with.

The cost savings gained by distributing the new currency in storage in Culpeper, and replacing it with used currency, was substantial enough to warrant a test of the idea. As a result, used currency not fit for circulation was "wrapped" in plastic sheeting and transported to Culpeper, rather than being destroyed. And the new currency stored in Culpeper was distributed to the Reserve Banks to replenish their supplies.

What happened?

The used currency smelled so badly that it had to be removed and destroyed, and replaced with new currency.

I'm sure you have come across some notes that are in bad shape. Picture an entire vault of such notes, that are sweat-soaked, stained, soft, and gnarled. The odor is indeed nauseating.

Heavy Money

Coins are produced by the U.S. Mint from thirteen-inch-wide, 1,500-feet-long strips of metal that they special-order. The coins are punched out as round discs on a press, heated to soften the metal, and run through a washer and a dryer to give the metal a shiny new appearance. They are then sent through a press that creates the "lip" that you can feel on a coin at its edge. Afterward, they are sent through a press which simultaneously strikes the images and information found on both sides of a coin. They are then inspected, and counted and placed into canvas bags and sewn shut. These bags of coins are then stored on pallets in a vault and shipped by armored trucks from the U.S. Mint in Philadelphia and Denver to Federal Reserve banks upon their request for more coins.

The Fed buys coins from the U.S. Mint at face value. Since the Mint can manufacture coins for a lesser cost than face value, the Mint makes a profit on coins. In 2005, its profit was $730 million.

But in 2006, the penny cost more to produce than its face value, about 1.23 cents; so did the nickel, about 5.73. This reduced the Mint's profit by $45 million in 2006, and continues to do so.

This type of situation creates a dilemma for the Mint, because it becomes possible to melt coins for a profit by extracting the metals used in its productions. So what the mint attempts to do is change the composition of metals used in the coin's production to reduce manufacturing costs below face value. This probably can be done for both the penny and the nickel. However, elimination of the penny has been discussed for at least four decades. Maybe this will be the catalyst for its demise.

Unlike currency, a coin is moved by armored trucks to Fed Banks instead of by air, because of the weight of the coin. A coin is also moved by armored trucks between Fed banks and their customers.

The Fed banks made payments of 61.5 billion coins, worth $6 billion, to depository institutions in 2003, and received 48.1 billion coins worth $4.9 billion, from them. All payments of coins to depository institutions and receipts of coins from them are debited and credited to their reserve accounts or clearing balance accounts, as in the case of currency. The same 10,300 financial institutions that deal directly with the Fed, for their currency needs, do so for coins also—and provide coin services to the other 8,700 depository institutions in the nation through correspondent arrangements.

As you would expect, the coin has a very lengthy life in circulation.

7

The Rise and Fall of the Check

If you have a checking account and use checks to make payments—and most people do since about 31 billion were written in 2005—it is interesting to go behind the scenes of the banking industry to see what happens to your check after it is received by the party to whom you are making the payment. The amount of resources that are expended in effecting the transaction and moving money from your checking account to that party's checking account may surprise you.

There are two parties to every check that is written, a "payor" and a "payee." You, as the originator of the check, are the payor, and the party to whom you are making the payment is the payee. (The payee can endorse the check over to a third party, who then becomes the payee in the transaction, and thus replaces the original payee.)

All of the checks that you write can be categorized into two groupings: (1) out-of-area checks, and (2) in-area checks.

Out of Area

An out-of-area check means that the party to whom you are making a payment, the payee, is located in a region serviced by a Fed office that is not the Fed office that services the region in which you, the payor, are located.

For example, you write and mail a check to a Boston firm to pay for clothing that you purchased, but you live in Chicago.

The Boston firm receives your check in the mail and deposits it into its checking account along with all of the other checks received that day.

Let's focus on your check, and what it takes to get money from your checking account into the Boston firm's checking account.

The Boston firm's bank will conditionally credit the Boston firm's account for the amount of your check after it is deposited. (The Boston firm may not have immediate access to the funds represented by your check, but may be able to withdraw such funds one day or perhaps two days later.)

The Boston firm's bank will transport your check to the Boston Fed office, that day, via surface transportation, and deposit it there. The Boston Fed will process your check, and credit the reserve account of the bank for the amount of your check. Such funds will be available to the bank in its reserve account the following morning.

The Boston Fed will also debit the interoffice settlement account of the Chicago Fed for the amount of your check.

The Boston Fed will then transport your check to the airport late that evening, via surface transportation. Your check will be loaded on board a Fed-chartered aircraft, and flown to Chicago.

Your check will then be transported, via surface transportation, from the Chicago airport to the Chicago Fed office early the next morning. The Chicago Fed will process your check, debit the reserve account of your bank for the amount of your check, and transport your check to your bank that morning. Your bank will debit your account for your check that day.

The Chicago Fed will also credit the interoffice settlement account of the Boston Fed for the amount of your check.

The above occurs each and every time you make an out-of-area check payment. All of these resources are expended on your behalf, and at no cost to you. Your check's value is always "at par," meaning it is not discounted in any way to pay for all of the above. This was not always the case. As late as 1966, 94 percent of commercial banks exchanged checks at par.

The other 6 percent "discounted" checks to cover processing costs.

Your cash balance in your checking account is an earning asset for your bank. Your bank earns a sufficient amount from the checking account balances that it has on deposit to absorb the costs of the above mentioned transportation, processing, and accounting, to pay the Fed for the services it renders, and to enjoy a profit.

In Area

An in-area check means that the party to whom you are making a payment, the payee, is in the same Fed office territory that you are in—as the payor. Therefore, your check does not have to be flown from one Fed office to another, and the amount of your check is not included in the Fed's interoffice settlement.

For example, you pay your electric bill to a local provider with a check. The electric company deposits your check with its bank the day it is received, and its account is credited for the amount. The bank transports your check to the Chicago Fed that same day. The Chicago Fed processes the check, and that same day, credits the reserve account of the electric company's bank, debits the reserve account of your bank, and transports the check to your bank early the next morning. Your bank then debits your checking account for the amount of your check.

Clearing House

The Fed's services that are described in the above examples of out-of-area and in-area check payments are known in banking as "check clearing and settlement."

This is contrasted with "demand deposit accounting," which your bank does for you with respect to your checking account. It adds money to your account when you make a deposit, subtracts from your account the amount of checks you write, and notifies you monthly of the status of your account.

About 40 percent of the checks written in our nation are cleared and settled by the Fed. In 2005, the Fed cleared and settled 12.6 billion checks having a total value of $14.7 trillion. "Clearing houses" that are operated by the banks and other financial institutions in a given geographic region that participate in these arrangements clear the remainder. Many cities in our country have an established clearing house.

These clearing houses perform the same "clearing" services as the Fed. They (1) arrange for the transportation of checks from banks to the clearing house; (2) keep a record of the total amount of dollars owed to each bank from their deposits of checks; (3) sort these checks by the paying banks; (4) keep a record of how much is owed by each bank for the checks written against accounts in their banks; and (5) arrange for transportation of the checks to the paying bank. The clearing houses will also arrange for transport of the checks to other clearing houses or Fed offices if the paying bank is out of the area, and will do the related accounting.

"Settlement" for the dollars involved, however, is done on Fed books.

Each business day, the clearing house computes a "net settlement" for all banks and other financial depositories participating as members of the clearing house." "Net settlement" means that each participant in the clearing house will end the day in one of three conditions: (1) owing money because the dollar amount of checks written against checking accounts in the bank exceeded the dollar amount of checks deposited by that bank for collection; (2) receiving money because the reverse is true; or (3) breaking even.

The "net settlement" position for each financial institution participating in the clearing house is given to the local Fed office. It's reserve account or clearing balance with the Fed is debited or credited accordingly through the Fed's Net Settlement Services. In 2005, the Fed processed more than 440,000 entries for such arrangements, including clearing houses.

How do banks and other financial depositories decide whether to use the Fed's check clearing and settlement services or to use the check clearing services of the clearing house? This decision is based solely upon the economics of the situation. Whichever alternative is more cost-effective will be the one used.

Two reasons for using the clearing house instead of the Fed may be that it is less costly to do so, or perhaps, the clearing house has a later deposit deadline. This decision will vary from day to day. Some days the Fed will be used, some days the clearing house will be used, and still other days both will be used.

For example, some clearing houses will clear all of the checks drawn on local payor banks, and will use the Fed for those drawn on out-of-area payor banks.

Six Critical Numbers

The Magnetic Ink Character Recognition (MICR) line is found at the bottom of the face of your check. This line contains most of the information the banking industry requires, in computer-readable form, to successfully provide checking account services to the entire nation. And to do so virtually error free.

Think of it. Billions of pieces of paper moving about the country each year, and every one of them accurately moving funds from a payor to a payee—with a margin for error so small that you may never experience it in your entire lifetime.

The technology that permits this is not new—it has been around for decades.

When you order checks from your bank, the MICR line—which is printed on the bottom of each check with "magnetized ink," so it can be accurately read by the computers and sorters used by the banking industry—contains:

1. your bank's ABA number, a unique number identifying it to the banking industry;

2. your account number, a unique number within your bank, identifying you as the owner of the checking account; and

3. a sequence number, each one being unique to a particular check.

These three numbers, when combined, make each check that you write a unique payment instrument in the nation, and in the world. These numbers, as a group, will not be duplicated by anyone.

There are three other numbers that are necessary for the efficient operation of the check system: (1) the amount of your check; (2) the ABA number of the depositing bank; and (3) the checking account number of the payee to whom you are making payment. These three numbers are captured by the banking system in the process of clearing and settling your check.

The bank that receives your check as a deposit (usually the bank of the payee to whom you are making a payment) is responsible for an MICR encoding of the amount of your check. This amount is encoded as the last item on the MICR line of your check. Both the Fed and privately operated clearing houses require the amount to have an MICR encoding before that check will be accepted by them for clearing and settlement.

Alternately, the depositing bank can pay a fee to the Fed or to the clearing house to do an MICR encoding of the amount of the check. Almost universally, banks do MICR encoding of the dollar amount themselves because it is less costly to do so.

The ABA number of the depositing bank (the payee's bank)—which is the fifth number essential for the efficient operation of the check system—is captured by the Fed or check clearing house when items are deposited with them for clearing and settlement.

The depositing bank will prepare a cash letter to accompany the items it is depositing for collection, and that cash letter will contain the ABA number of the depositing bank as well as a listing of all checks, the total dollar amount, and the total number of checks in the cash letter.

The sixth and final number required for the efficient operation of the check system is the checking account number of the payee, which is captured by the payee's bank from the deposit slip of the payee.

With these six numbers, the banking system has all of the information it needs, in computer-readable form, to effect the movement of funds from payor to payee—efficiently and error free.

A Second Line

Occasionally, you may notice that one of your canceled checks that has been returned to you by your bank, after it has been paid, contains a second MICR line that has been appended to the bottom of the check.

This means that one of the banks that handled that check in the process of clearing and settlement, either a Fed bank or a commercial bank, was unable to read one or more of the four numbers contained in the MICR line. It, therefore was required to "repair" the MICR line, by re-encoding the four numbers and attaching that repaired MICR line to the bottom of your check. This "repairing" allows your check to be processed by automated equipment throughout the banking system, as opposed to being manually handled as an "exception" item, at far greater cost.

Modernizing The System

In the early 1970s, George Mitchell initiated a dramatic modernization of our nation's check system. He did so as chairman of the Board's Committee on the Payments Mechanism, extensively utilizing the "pyramid" structure described in chapter 4.

This was accomplished concurrently with the modernization of Fedwire, as discussed in chapter 5.

Problems

The two major problems confronting the nation's check system were (1) the length of time required for payment to be completed when using a check as a payment instrument, and (2) Federal Reserve check "float." The former was a consumer issue, and the latter a Fed issue.

Consumer Issue

At the time the modernization of our nation's check system was initiated, only 15 percent of checks were written, cleared, and settled overnight. This means that when you, as a payee, deposited checks into your checking account, only 15 percent of such checks would be credited to your account—and funds made available to you for withdrawal—within twenty-four hours. The delay for credit and funds availability on the other 85 percent of checks deposited into your account was up to twelve days or more.

Such a delay was a function of the location of the payor's bank, the dollar amount of the check, and other factors—including the bank's taking advantage of the situation at the expense of its customer, the payee.

The threshold for when credit and funds availability should have been given to its customer is when the bank itself received credit and funds availability from the Fed.

If the bank gave credit and funds availability prior to it receiving such, it would be in an exposed position if the check was not honored and paid by the payor's bank. This could happen, for example, if the payor's account did not have sufficient funds.

If, on the other hand, the bank gave credit and funds availability to its customer after it received such from the Fed, it was profiting at its customer's expense. It had use of the funds for a period of time prior to making these available for withdrawal by the customer.

The credit and funds availability schedules that banks gave to its customers for their deposits were complex and convoluted. In many cases, banks were taking advantage of the situation and profiting at customer's expense.

Moreover, the longer it took for final payment to be made on a check, the easier it was for dishonest persons to conduct check "kiting" and other schemes.

In a check-kiting scheme, the perpetrator writes a check against an account in bank A, then writes a check against an account in bank B and deposits it in bank A to cover the first check written, and then writes a check against an account in bank C and deposits it in bank B to cover the second check written, etc.

Shortening the time required for final payment to be effected when using the check as a payment instrument would place a severe handicap on perpetrators of check-kiting schemes.

Float

What is Fed check float?

It occurs when the Fed credits the reserve accounts of depositing banks for the dollar amounts of the checks they deposit with the Fed for collection—before the Fed can process, transport, and present those same checks to the paying banks and debit their reserve accounts. In essence, the Fed inflates bank reserves by the total amount of the credits to the depositing banks. These bank reserves are investable assets and create income for the recipients.

Why did the Fed permit check float? Why did it not delay crediting for deposits until it was able to debit for collections from paying banks?

126

The answer is that the Fed desired to provide a level of "certainty" to our nation's check system.

Banks were withholding availability of funds from consumers on their check deposits into their checking accounts. In certain extreme cases, withholding availability of funds for up to seven to ten days was justified—because the paying bank was far distant and isolated. But the extreme case quickly became the norm—and delayed availability of seven to ten days became common.

The Fed set its availability schedule to preclude banks from "hiding behind" the extreme-case argument. The Fed, in essence, said to the banks, "Here is our availability schedule to you on your check deposits with us. No matter where the paying bank is located, if you give us your checks for collection, we will pass credit to you on your check deposits not later than three days after we receive your deposit." The Fed knew that it would not be able to collect on all of the checks deposited with it in this period of time, but—in the interests of providing certainty in availability of funds and thus precluding banks from taking advantage of consumers—decided that the creation of Fed check float was a lesser evil than the continuation of the extreme delayed availability practices of banks. Banks could no longer justify such practices after the Fed established "certainty" in availability of funds.

Over time, average daily Fed check float grew to a very sizable number—billions of dollars. Shortening the time required to collect checks from paying banks became desirable, as this would decrease the level of Fed check float.

Regional Check Processing Center (RCPC)

The Fed initiated the RCPC program in the early 1970s to increase the number of checks cleared in the nation on an overnight basis.

Prior to implementation of this program, each of the twelve Fed Banks and twenty-five Fed Branches cleared and settled checks. A study was undertaken, and a computer model was developed by TRW under a contract with the Fed, to determine the most cost-efficient way to increase overnight check clearings. This was done under the auspices of the Board's Committee on the Payments Mechanism, chaired by vice chairman Mitchell, and supported by the Conferences of First Vice Presidents and Presidents of the Federal Reserve banks. Appropriate committees, subcommittees, and task forces were organized under these conferences and assignments were made.

After considerable study and analysis, including extensive use of the TRW computer model, the following conclusions and recommendations made their way up the pyramid structure for final approval by the Board.

1. Each of the twelve Fed Banks and twenty five Branches was to expand its overnight check-clearing zones, to an extent that would permit the maximum number of checks to be cleared and settled consistent with reasonable costs and the maximum reduction in Fed check float.

2. Thirteen new Fed check-clearing and settlement offices, called "RCPCs," were to be opened throughout the nation, to complement those activities in the Fed banks and branches. It was more cost efficient to add these thirteen new facilities than it was to expand the overnight clearing zones of the Fed banks and branches to cover these newly established overnight clearing zones.

3. Surface and air transportation services were to be expanded to accommodate these newly established overnight clearing zones.

4. Additional resources—both people and equipment; including computers and check sorters, were to be added as required.

Nationwide implementation of the above four major recommendations became known in the Fed, and in the banking industry, as the "RCPC program."

Each of the 12 Fed Banks began implementation of this program in their respective Fed Districts. Some moved faster than others, and more than once, Mitchell brought in the slow movers for "encouragement."

When nationwide implementation of this program was completed, which occurred in the late 1970s, over 85 percent of the checks written in the nation were cleared and settled on an overnight basis. This compared with just 15 percent being cleared and settled on an overnight basis before implementation of the program.

As a result, Fed check float was reduced to a very small number (today, average daily Fed check float amounts to a few hundred million dollars), availability of funds to consumers on their deposits into their checking accounts improved dramatically, and the opportunities for check kiting, and similar abuses of our nation's check system, were eliminated.

Funding of the RCPC program resulted in some interesting gyrations within the Fed.

The proposals for establishment of RCPCs were forwarded to the Board for approval. These were reviewed by the staff, and by Mitchell's Committee on the Payments Mechanism, and placed on the Board's "consent calendar" for full Board approval.

One day I received a phone call from Dave Melnicoff, who, at the time, was the staff director at the Board, and he asked me to meet with him. He informed me that Chairman Burns desired to be briefed on the status of the RCPC program. I prepared a briefing, went over it with Dave; we fine-tuned it, and scheduled a meeting with Burns through his secretary, Catherine Milardi.

After rescheduling the meeting a couple of times because of pressing matters attended to by Burns, we finally were able to brief him; it was an evening briefing.

When I got to the part in the briefing about the costs incurred in implementing the RCPCs that were operational at that time, Burns said to me, "Mr. Kudlinski, how much did you say we have spent on these so far?"

I said, "Mr. chairman, to date the one-time costs have been $30 million and the incremental recurring annual costs are $30 million." He appeared surprised, particularly, since all of this was approved on the consent calendar without full Board discussion of the matter.

He then said to me, "Mr. Kudlinski, from now on, nothing goes on the consent calendar if it costs even one dollar. And before you schedule any item requiring the expenditure of dollars on the action calendar, I want to be briefed on it." Virtually all proposals involving the expenditure of dollars by the Fed banks came to my office since I was the director of the Division of Federal Reserve Bank Operations.

We emerged from the briefing at 8 P.M.

Of course, I informed Mitchell the next morning about the briefing and he just smiled and said, "The full Board approved the total RCPC program, but if the chairman wants us to discuss each RCPC proposal, that's OK."

Burns, as mentioned earlier, looked upon the Fed as the custodian of the public purse. And, among other matters, he believed that $60 million was too large an amount to be spent without full Board discussion, review, and approval—and wanted the record to show that.

In any event, the very next proposal that came into my office requiring the expenditure of dollars was from the Boston Fed. Dutifully, I made an appointment to brief Burns on the matter.

I entered his office in the late afternoon, and he looked tired.

Burns worked seven days a week as Fed chairman, and normally didn't leave his office until after 8 P.M., Monday through Friday.

I had some meetings with him on Saturdays, and when I left in the mid-afternoon, he was still there.

His wife, Helen, told me that he slept no longer than three

to four hours each night—he was one of those individuals that did not require much sleep.

As I walked into his office, Burns was sitting on his sofa, had his pipe in his hand, and there were papers covering the small table in front of his sofa from his previous meeting.

He looked up and said to me, "Mr. Kudlinski, why are you here?"

I said, "Mr. chairman, I'm here to brief you on the kitchen equipment for the new building for the Federal Reserve Bank of Boston."

He paused and then said, "Why are you doing this?"

I said, "Because it costs three-hundred-sixty-five thousand dollars and you wanted to be briefed on anything requiring the expenditure of dollars that is scheduled for the action calendar."

He said, "Mr. Kudlinski, what do you think I know about kitchen equipment?"

I said, "About the same things I know, Mr. chairman."

He said, "Well, has anyone looked at this who knows something about kitchen equipment?" I said," Yes, sir, our consultants, and they believe that the expenditure is reasonable and appropriate."

He said, "Very well."

And that was the end of the meeting.

Subsequently, I had additional meetings with Burns on proposed Fed bank expenditures, and other matters. After a time, he sensed that I would always give him the facts, no matter if these were favorable to what we were attempting to do, or unfavorable. And our relationship became one of mutual trust. He knew that I would remove all Fed politics from anything I told him or briefed him on. And that I always told him the truth.

That is why, on the photo that Burns personalized for me at my request when he left the Fed, he wrote, "In warm admiration of your scholarship and your personal character."

He mentioned scholarship in the caption because I received my Ph.D. while being employed at the Board. Three of us on the Board's staff, John Denkler, Warren Minami, and I, all received our doctorates at the same time. We had a party at the Fort Myers Officers Club. (John Denkler was a retired Navy captain, and thus we could take advantage of officer-club pricing for the party.) We invited Chairman Burns and his wife, and many others—and they were kind enough to attend. Officers' clubs are now a thing of the past in the military.

The Fed Air Force

In implementing the RCPC program, the twelve Fed banks, twenty five Fed branches, and thirteen RCPCs all became "hubs." Thus, there were fifty hubs in the nationwide RCPC network. Surface and air transportation had to be scheduled and arranged for each of these fifty hubs.

Starting in the late afternoon, surface couriers began to pick up check deposits at the financial institutions farthest from the local Fed office, and worked their way inward, picking up checks from banks closer in, eventually delivering all such deposits to the Fed offices. Thus, the farther away a financial institution was from the Fed office, the earlier it had to have its deposit ready for courier pick up. And many surface couriers were required to service the banks in each hub area.

Each of these hubs, in turn, outsorted out-of-area checks (checks drawn on paying banks in the other forty-nine hubs) and transported these to an airport.

The Fed chartered a substantial number of aircraft to move these checks among the fifty hubs nationwide—including propeller and jet aircraft, single-engine and multiengine planes. We, in the Fed, referred to this large number of chartered aircraft as the "Fed air force."

Scheduling of outbound and inbound flights from and to each hub is complex. There were 200 Fed chartered flights, transporting 50,000 pounds of checks each night. That amounted to twenty-five tons of checks each night. The airport that each aircraft took off from on its outbound leg was the airport at which the aircraft would terminate its flight on its inbound leg.

Each aircraft would make one or more stops on its outbound leg and on its inbound leg, and at each such stop, checks would be dropped off and picked up at the hubs along its route. Those that were dropped off would be loaded on to other planes flying to other hubs in which the paying banks were located. Those that were picked up would be flown by that aircraft to hubs along its route in which the paying banks were located.

There were five main hubs where primary check exchanges took place: Philadelphia, Atlanta, Cincinnati, Dallas, and Chicago. When each aircraft completed its nightly schedule and landed at the end of the night in its terminating airport, the only checks remaining on that aircraft would be those drawn on the paying banks serviced by the hub in that city.

Those checks would be transported from the airport to the local hub, sorted according to each paying bank, and transported by surface couriers to the paying banks. In essence, the surface couriers would be reversing the routes that they used when transporting check deposits into the hub.

Aircraft in the Fed air force had accidents, and crashes have occurred. In such instances, cash letters were reconstructed from computer records and clearing and settlement were delayed.

The Letter

While the RCPC program was in the process of being implemented, a historical event occurred that provides a "feel" for the culture that existed in the Fed.

Board staff members regularly evaluate the operations of the twelve Fed banks and their branches and the RCPCs. The division that I directed was responsible for such evaluation. We conducted operations reviews and examinations of the banks on a regular basis and, in addition, had access to a very detailed database for evaluation.

We determined that twelve Fed offices (hubs) in the nationwide RCPC network were not doing a very good job in their check-clearing and settlement operations. We presented the matter to the Board's Committee on Federal Reserve Bank Activities (now known as the Board's Committee on Federal Reserve Bank Affairs), chaired at that time by Jack Sheehan, along with a draft letter to be sent to each of the offices, telling them to correct the problems. The committee agreed, the matter was taken up by the full Board, and the letters were approved and sent to the offices.

And then "the shit hit the fan," so to speak.

To my knowledge, this was the first formal letter of its kind—chastising twelve Fed offices for performance and telling them to correct the situation—that had been sent by the Board to the Fed banks. This type of thing previously had been done with a "gentleman's" phone call, quietly and discreetly—with varied results. They were not accustomed to being criticized—and having their "dirty laundry" aired.

Some Fed offices, notably the New York offices responded with a scathing letter addressed to me, and listing all of the things that make check-clearing and settlement operations difficult in Manhattan, including one-way streets impeding check couriers. Others stayed silent.

But the tactic worked. The twelve Fed offices corrected their problems, although I must admit, the temperature among the Fed banks was somewhat cooler toward me for a time.

And I'll bet that a similar letter has not been sent since.

Today's System

In the early 1990s, technological advancements in communications, networking, and check-sorting equipment made it possible for the Fed to centralize computer operations supporting its check-processing services in one of its three mainframe centers in New York (East Rutherford, New Jersey), Dallas, and Richmond. Check sorters in the Fed offices currently providing clearing and settlement services are all driven by that one mainframe computer center. The other two centers provide backup capability. (The Fed prefers that the services driven by each of the three facilities not be publicly disclosed, for security reasons.)

Prior to the 1990s, each Fed bank had a computer mainframe driving the check sorters in its district, and Fed branches and RCPCs also were so equipped, particularly early on in the RCPC program.

In 2003, there were forty-five hubs in the Fed's nationwide check-clearing network processing paper checks. By year's end, 2004, the number was reduced to thirty-two, and by 2008 there were eighteen. Now there are only two, in Cleveland and Chicago.

Part of the reason for such a reduction is that the Fed's check volume has decreased considerably since 2002. The Fed reduced the number of hubs because it made economic sense to do so. Paper check volume has decreased substantially because of the truncation of the paper check at the first bank of deposit and its conversion to an electronic item—this is done through the Check 21 System, which is described later. Also, consumers are using alternate payment means, including the ACH and other electronic payment systems, such as those supporting point-of-sale and check conversion to electronic payments; and the proliferation in bank mergers, creating huge money centers and regional banks, has resulted in a lot of checks now being cleared as "on-us" items that previously were "interbank" items.

With regard to the former, ACH annual volume grew to 14 billion payments in 2005—a sizeable number—and represented about 45 percent of total check volume. Moreover, when all electronic payments were taken into account, electronic payment volume exceeded our nation's annual check volume for the first time. We are certain that is the case today.

Nationwide, check volume peaked in the mid-1990s at about 50 billion items annually. The last time the Fed surveyed the banking industry to determine check volume was in 2003, at which time it was 36 billion items. It is substantially less today.

The transition away from check usage is being driven by economics. A check costs the Fed five cents to clear and settle, and the banking industry about eight cents to process. An ACH item costs the Fed one cent to clear and settle and the banking industry about one cent to process. Electronic payments are substantially less expensive.

With regard to the impact of bank mergers on our nation's check volume, more than 25 percent of checks that are deposited today are drawn on the financial institution in which they are deposited and are called "on-us" items. This is a significant change from what previously was the case prior to all of these bank mergers.

All of the transitions in our nation's payments mechanism from paper to electronic payments was predicted by George Mitchell, first as a Board member, and later as the Fed vice chairman. During his entire fifteen-year Board career, almost all of his public speaking focused on the advantages that we are now enjoying from the more efficient electronic means of making payments.

Check 21

The banking industry announced, in late 2004, its plan to begin truncating checks. The front and back sides of checks were converted to electronic images, and those were sent through the clearing and settlement system to effect the final payment. This is done just as clearing and settlement now take place for paper checks, except the items are in electronic form rather than paper. Paper checks are costly to move about the country by surface and air transportation and to process to effect final payments. It is less expensive to move and process electronic images, much like ACH items are now being cleared and settled.

Congress passed a law in 2003 that provides the legal framework for check truncation. Any bank in the clearing and settlement process can truncate a check—which means they create an electronic image of the check and destroy the paper check. However, if any bank or customer of a bank desires a paper copy, the electronic image can be used to create a legally acceptable copy of the check.

The Fed's role in check truncation is exactly the same as it is in the paper check system. Depository institutions are able to send the electronic images resulting from check truncation to the Fed, and the Fed clears and settles such items, just as it does in the paper check system described earlier—thus effecting final payment. In 2005, 25.2 percent of all checks presented to the paying bank by the Fed were in electronic form instead of paper. Now the percentage is much greater.

Check truncation is not a new idea. It has been bantered about in the banking industry for the past fifty years. But until recently, the technology required to perform the function at an affordable price was not available. Advancements in wideband communications and check-processing technology have made it possible to convert the front and back sides of a check to an electronic image, and to transmit that image through the clearing and settlement system to effect a final payment at a cost that is less than is required to do the same for the paper check. Of course, scale economies apply—so large volumes are required to enjoy the cost-benefit advantages of check truncation.

And what are these benefits?

With mature volumes, depository institutions save considerable dollars when compared to the cost that they have to bear to clear and settle a like amount of paper checks. Consumers enjoy earlier funds availability on their check deposits. In today's check system, consumers have access to the funds they deposit by checks in one to three days. This is shortened to one day or less in Check 21.

Consumers have to be aware that check truncation removes "float" time that they enjoyed when writing checks. They no longer are able to write checks and assume they have one, two, or three days to get money into their checking accounts to cover the items before these reach their banks for payment. Check truncation means that the item will be presented to your bank for payment the same day that you write it. If the funds are not in your account, you could be subject to hefty overdraft fees.

Check truncation, in reality, is a step on the way to debit card usage exclusively, in which your payments will be immediately deducted from your account at the time of your purchase. Under current rules, it is more preferable to use a credit card rather than a debit card (or a check, for that matter) for all your payments—provided you pay the balance due each and every month. In this manner you can make use of your bank's money for up to thirty days free of charge; in essence a "free" float to you, and you also enjoy ancillary benefits—such as credit for free airline travel based upon the amount charged to your credit card.

Fed Headquarters

Arthur Burns

To Jim Kudlinski — with appreciation to my Fed associate — and best wishes — Bill Miller

Bill Miller

To Jim Kudlinski
With thanks and best wishes for valiant services
—Paul Volcker

Paul Volcker

Alan Greenspan

Ben Bernanke

George Mitchell, Vice Chairman under Burns

Biggest Table in Washington

8

High Profile Building Program

Fed Building

The Fed program for replacing its buildings is controlled by the Board. The Division of Reserve Bank Operations and Payment Systems (formerly known as the Division of Federal Reserve Bank Operations and budgets) provides all of the staffing to the Board on this program. When a Fed bank desires to replace one or more of its buildings, it relies upon the Building Program staff in this division to advise them and to take them through the entire process. Specific requirements are set forth for all of the steps in the process, the major ones being:

>space planning and building footprinting
>study of alternatives to meeting space requirements
>site selection
>architect hiring
>design of the building
>construction firm hiring
>planning and construction for the building
>construction of the building
>outfitting of the building

The Fed bank hires various consultants to assist in these steps, with the advice and consent of the Building Program staff. Each of the above major steps results in a proposal being forwarded to Headquarters for approval. Each proposal is re-

viewed first by Board staff, then by the Board's Federal Reserve Bank Affairs Committee, and then by the full Board.
Thus, numerous Board reviews and approvals are required before a new Fed building is constructed and available for occupancy.

Politics

As soon as word gets out that the Fed is planning construction
of a new building, politics enters into the equation. The local
community, of course, attempts to influence the entire process.
The fact that the Building Program is so very disciplined—that
is, specific requirements are set forth and proposals for each
major step must be prepared and submitted to the Board for
approval—helps in combating the well-meaning but not neces-
sarily cost-effective intentions of the local community. In all
cases, the most efficient and cost-effective solutions must be
chosen, and the Fed is able to "hang its hat" on that requirement in dealing with the politics.

The politics can be illustrated by reviewing some aspects of
the Kansas City Fed's announcement in May 2003 that it
planned to construct a new bank building in Kansas City, Missouri.

It became known that the bank was interested in a site just
to the south of the downtown area. (The bank's current building is located in the downtown area.) The local community,
however, and the civic leaders therein wanted the bank to select a site in the downtown area of the city—and specifically, in
a proposed revitalization area. The reasoning was that the Fed
would provide an "anchor" and act as a catalyst for redevelopment in the area.

The bank's preferred site was larger and less costly than
the site preferred by the civic leaders.

I was contacted by a reporter at the *Kansas City Star* about
this matter just prior to the date that the Kansas City Fed was
going to officially announce its site selection. The reporter told

me that virtually everyone with an interest in Kansas City wanted the Fed to locate its new building downtown. The mayor, city planners, and prominent local bankers, including the two Kemper families with control of the UMB and Commerce banks, were among those civic leaders letting their desires be known and promising to lobby the Kansas City Fed.

I told the reporter that, unfortunately, the Kansas City Fed cannot select the downtown site because it is more expensive and does not provide as effective a solution. The Fed is required to select the most cost-effective and efficient site. Nothing in the Federal Reserve Act authorizes the Fed to engage in, nor promote, downtown redevelopment. I ended my conversation with the reporter by telling him, "You cannot lobby these things politically, you have to prove it economically."

The reporter also questioned how the Kansas City Fed could select a site since they had not yet hired an architect or designed the building. He stated, "How do they know if either of the two sites can accommodate the size of the building required?" I told him that their space plan, in essence, provided them with the "footprint" for the building. From this they knew the size of the building required.

A few days later, the Kansas City Fed announced the site just south of the downtown area as the location of its new building—and this location was reported to the Board in Washington for final approval. And that is where the building is located today.

The reaction from the civic leaders was as expected.

Jonathan Kemper, president and CEO of Commerce Bank, expressed disappointment by stating, "They've consistently left us in the dark." R. Crosby Kemper III, President and CEO of UMB Bank, said, "This is a real slap at the community. It shows an imperial attitude," reported the *Kansas City Star,* on May 24, 2003.

What went on in Kansas City has occurred in every Fed city in the nation when a new Fed building program is or has been announced. Much of this local community anxiety could be avoided if civic leaders understood that their local Fed was obligated to select the most cost-effective and cost-efficient solution—and that it must ignore all other aspects.

Building Boom

The Fed's investment in its buildings nationwide totals $2.6 billion. At year's end, 2005, the investment remaining on its balance sheet was $1.8 billion, net of depreciation.

Starting in the 1970s and continuing to this day, a building boom has been going on in the Fed. Currently, there are five new building programs under way in Houston, Detroit, Seattle, Kansas City, and Little Rock. When Fed buildings approach forty years in age, new construction is required to replace these buildings for a variety of reasons, including accommodation of new technology in Fed operations.

It is interesting to review what has taken place during this building boom—and what didn't take place. Let's start with the latter.

New York

The New York Fed's building program had been under way for approximately ten years when I became involved with it in the mid-1970s.

The New York Fed had purchased a building on a site across the street from the Bank's original building—which it was occupying and planned to retain. A period of ten years had elapsed—during which time the New York Fed had been engaged in buying up leases from the tenants in the purchased building, and in demolishing the building. When I got involved in the project, approximately $10 million had been expended in buying up leases, and all but a corner of the purchased building had been demolished. A tailor occupying leased space in this corner was demanding an unreasonable amount for vacating his lease—and the bank decided to build around him. When his lease expired, that corner would be demolished, and new construction would be completed on that corner.

The site upon which the New York Fed was planning to build a 750,000-gross-square-feet office tower annex was hampered by "view corridor restrictions," which required construction of a building supported by 100 foot tall columns. These would necessitate special shielding to preclude exposure to an explosive or other type of attack upon the columns.

A below-ground "operations complex" was to be constructed underneath the building to house the bank's check-processing, currency and coin, computer, and loading-dock facilities.

There was a historically significant Methodist church on one end of the site, which was to remain—and which caused additional construction problems. Because of the small size of the site, and lack of space to store construction materials, tight scheduling of the assemblage of materials and construction would be required.

As a result, construction costs were projected at $250 million, which made it the most costly building project ever undertaken by the Fed.

The Building Program staff at the Board, headed by Walt Althausen, an architect, and consisting of construction planners, engineers, and people with similar backgrounds, had determined that the building was too expensive and that there were less costly alternatives available for meeting the New York Fed's space needs. The Board's Committee on Federal Reserve Bank Activities, chaired by Jack Sheehan, and the full Board, agreed with this analysis and supported additional study of alternatives.

A meeting was arranged with the Building Committee of the New York Fed's Board of Directors to inform them of this decision. Jack Sheehan, Ron Burke, who was then the director of the Division of Federal Reserve Bank Operations (and whom I later succeeded as director), and I flew to New York as the Board's representatives.

The Building Committee of the New York Fed's Board consisted of David Rockefeller, who was chairman of the committee (and also chairman of the Chase Bank), Roswell Gilpatric, an attorney who was prominent during the Kennedy Administration, and a gentleman by the name of Frank Milliken, who was the CEO of Kennecott Copper.

We arrived at the New York Fed and were escorted to their boardroom by Tom Timlen, a senior vice president (and subsequently the first vice president of the bank). This is when the "maneuvering" planned by the New York Fed for the meeting materialized.

Tom escorted Jack Sheehan to the Board table, and he then escorted Ron Burke and I to the "visitor" seats. These were situated such that you could observe what was going on at the Board table, but you could not participate in the discussion.

In walked Rockefeller, Gilpatric, and Milliken; they took their seats across the table from Sheehan, and the meeting began.

The posturing for this meeting by the New York Fed was quite clever. By seating Burke and me in the visitors' gallery, they had a three to one advantage at the table. Moreover, they didn't want their Board members to deal with two staff from Washington. Instead, they would deal only with "Governor" Sheehan.

David Rockefeller did most of the talking for the New York Fed.

He began by stating displeasure with the timing of the Board of Governors' objections to the New York building program—namely, ten years after its inception, and after $10 million had been spent buying up leases. (These were valid objections.)

After being notified of the Board of Governors' decision to further study alternatives to meeting the space needs of the New York Fed, Rockefeller stated that the New York Fed would cooperate and participate in such studies—"only if it is clearly understood that the bank will proceed with planning for construction of the new building while it is participating in a study of alternatives." He stated further that the bank would not slow down its efforts in any way.

I was put on the front end of the study of alternatives as the Board of Governors' representative, and E. Gerald Corrigon was put on the front end as the New York Fed's representative.

Rockefeller went on to state that the Fed had an opportunity to do for New York City what the Chase Bank did for the city when it constructed Chase Plaza. At that time, he stated, New York was undergoing the same type of economic pressures that it currently was experiencing. The Chase Plaza project inserted millions of dollars into the New York economy and was helpful in turning things around. He made a very eloquent speech.

I couldn't help thinking at the time, however, that the Fed did not have a charter to perform such a revitalization function under the Federal Reserve Act.

We returned to Washington and the study of alternatives to meeting the New York Fed's space requirements began.

Gerry Corrigon was a formidable opponent. He is a very bright man, and has had a very successful career.

At the time this study of alternatives was initiated, Gerry was, as I recall, treasurer of the New York Fed. Al Hayes was president of the Bank, and Dick Debs was first vice president. Shortly thereafter, upon the retirement of Hayes, Paul Volcker was appointed president.

Gerry and Paul Volcker worked well together. When Volcker replaced Miller as chairman of the Fed, Gerry came to Washington with him as a special assistant. Gerry subsequently was appointed president of the Federal Reserve Bank of Minneapolis, and then president of the New York Fed. When Gerry left the Fed, he joined Paul Volcker at an investment banking house on Wall Street.

During the study of alternatives I had a meeting in my office in Washington with the man who was to build the new building for the New York Fed—whose name I cannot recall.

153

He proceeded to brief me on all of the buildings he had constructed, and it was a very impressive list.

He then asked me, "How many buildings have you constructed, Jim?"

I told him, "None, and I don't have to be a builder to tell you that the planned new construction for the New York Fed is too expensive."

I met with quite a few consultants for the New York Fed, and all were prominent in their field of expertise. I also had an opportunity to personally visit virtually all of the vacant office space in Manhattan.

At the time, in the mid 1970s, New York was under economic pressures. New York was experiencing a period of two to three years when financial and other corporations believed they could move out of the expensive New York district to less expensive areas and not be harmed, As a result, 4 million gross square feet of office space was vacant near or on Wall Street. I visited many of these locations. Office space could be had in the Wall Street area for $8.00 a square foot.

I also visited the Home Insurance building in Manhattan, in close proximity to the New York Fed. The building contained approximately 1 million gross square feet of space, and the New York Fed was leasing one-half of it.

It was during this time period that Gerry Corrigan came to my office with an analysis that showed that construction of the new building would be about $275 million less expensive in "life-cycle" costs than any alternative under consideration. I went through the numbers with him, and was not impressed—I could tell from the way he presented the material that he did not believe the numbers. Gerry knew that we at the Board were on the right side of this issue. That new building was too expensive.

The analysis was completed, the Board in Washington made its final decision, and the New York Fed's building program was terminated.

The Board recommended to New York that it purchase the Home Insurance building (it was offered to me for $37 million), and construct a below-ground operations center on the cleared site across the street from the original New York Fed building.

The New York Fed turned down the alternative, and subsequently asked the Board to allow them to pursue their original building plan "if it could be constructed for $90 million."

(We at the Board had arrived at a $75 million cost estimate to build a facility outside Manhattan that would be identical to what the bank was proposing, minus the 100-foot "stilts," and on a larger site. The bank asked the Board for $15 million more than that, and the Board approved the request.)

The New York Fed contemplated building a "poured concrete" facility in an attempt to bring costs down to $90 million, but it could not be done.

The New York Fed ultimately extended its lease of space at the Home Insurance building for 5 years at $8.00 a square foot, and sought a site outside Manhattan for an operations center.

Approximately two years later, the Home Insurance building was sold for a sum well over $100 million. Corporations had returned to New York, having recognized their mistake in moving out, real estate values had escalated, and the New York Fed's lease of space at $8.00 a square foot was looking good. But a purchase of the Home Insurance building would have looked even better.

Subsequently, New York refurbished its original bank building, and built an operations center in East Rutherford, New Jersey, in 1992 (which also houses one of the Fed's three main-frame computer centers). Chase Bank ultimately built an office complex on the vacant land across the street from the bank, known as Fed Center Plaza, and the New York Fed now leases a considerable amount of space in that building. (The New York Fed moved from the Home Insurance Building.)

Boston

Boston has the best-designed building in the entire Federal Reserve System. Frank Morris, then president of the Boston Fed, and Jim Mcintosh, then first vice president, did a good job with this building program in the mid-1970s. The all-in costs of the building were $107 million—a steal when compared to today's prices.

The building complex consists of a thirty-three-story office tower, and an operations center built mostly underground and adjacent to the tower.

The operations center houses the First Federal Reserve Districts' check-clearing and settlement, currency and coin, and computer operations, as well as vaults and loading-dock facilities.

The vaults in the operations center are enormous. When I first saw them, I told Jim Mcintosh that the New England Patriots could easily use the vaults as an indoor practice facility—they are the largest I have ever seen. A prototypical automated coin-handling system was installed inside the vaults as an experiment, at a cost of several million dollars.

Coinage is very heavy, and the system was designed to preclude manual handling of the weighty bags of coin. Upon the Fed's receipt of coinage, it is stored in a vault. The Fed then moves this coinage out of its vault to financial institutions, via surface courier, as it is ordered to meet the needs of the customers of banks, S&Ls, mutual savings banks, and credit unions.

There were numerous problems in debugging the prototype coin-handling system, and when I left the Fed in 1981, it was not operating properly. Eventually, it had to be abandoned.

If you fly into the Boston airport, the Fed building is easy to spot—particularly if the sun is shinning. It glimmers because sunlight is reflected from the façade of the tower.

Jim Mcintosh, who was the director of the Division of Federal Reserve Bank Operations at the Board prior to Burke and me, did a lot of traveling with Mitchell and me as he was assigned to work on payments-mechanism matters by the Conference of First Vice Presidents. Together, and including our wives, we saw a lot of Europe in our dealings with the Bank for

International Settlements and foreign central bankers, including Kevin Kearney.

Jim, a Fed colleague and a good friend of Mitchell's, Kevin Kearney's and mine, unfortunately passed away unexpectedly at an early age, and the Fed—and we all—lost a terrific man.

San Francisco

The twelfth Fed District's building program presented a unique problem that had not been experienced elsewhere in the Fed.

The building site selected was on Market Street in San Francisco, and construction occurred in the late 1970s.

Because of the hydrostatic pressure pushing upward from the soil in the area, the lower level of the building had to be tied down into bedrock to keep it from buckling upward.

The building is also unique because it contains a money museum depicting the history and evolution of money in our country.

The cost for design and construction of this display was $2.5 million, and John Balles, who was then president of the San Francisco Fed, very much appreciated our support in getting this project approved by the Board, including by Chairman Burns.

John knew that Burns considered himself the custodian of the public purse, and was not one to be frivolous with taxpayers' dollars.

John was also aware that Burns had just visited the San Francisco Fed—and upon his return to the Board, Burns called me to his office and asked, "Mr. Kudlinski, why are we constructing a new building in San Francisco? That is a fine old building."

I gave him the reasons, including lack of space for offices and operations, and antiquated support facilities—such as elevators, vaults, docks, and climate control. I told him that it is a fine forty-year-old building, and it will be sold and utilized by someone who can "fit" into the building. I was not sure he was convinced, but he accepted the rationale.

Now obviously, a money museum is neither critical nor essential to the operation of a Fed Bank. So how did we get this one past Burns and the rest of the Board?

It's how you "package" it that is important.

It became part of the "artwork" budget for the new building. Every new Fed building budget contains an amount for artwork, and San Francisco ended up with less art and a money museum.

If you are in San Francisco, stop in at the Fed on Market Street and visit the museum. You will find it quite interesting and worth your time.

Minneapolis

The Minneapolis Fed building was constructed in the 1960s. It was unique because of the system used to support the building, among other features, and it was an "architectural" award-winning building.

The building's support system consisted of steel cables on two sides of the elongated rectangular building—upon which the building was "hung." The cables actually supported the weight of the building.

Unfortunately, the support system and other parts of the building deteriorated prematurely and it had to be replaced in the 1980s, way before the time of its original projected life span.

Among the problems was a design error, which did not provide adequate leeway for expansion and contraction inside the building and externally on the facade of the building. Over time, seams had opened up on the facade as well as the interior of the building. As a result, the spaces between the double-paned windows were retaining and filling up with water. The building was also full of asbestos.

Interestingly, the Fed pursued litigation only against the

manufacturer of the asbestos products used in the building. The other potentially libelous parties were not pursued because of insufficient assets for recovery—should the Fed have been successful in its actions.

The building ultimately was sold to a developer who stripped it down to structural steel, and rebuilt the entire facility.

The replacement Minneapolis Fed building was constructed with the operational spaces forming the base of the building and occupying the lower floors. Office space was constructed on top of that. (All new Fed buildings are constructed similarly, following somewhat the design of the Boston Fed building.)

Ron Burke, who succeeded Jim Mcintosh as director of the Division of Federal Reserve Bank Operations at the Board, questioned the expected life span of the unique building support system in the vintage 1960s building shortly after he became director. And history proved him right. It didn't last.

Ron left the Board to become president and CEO of the Bank Administration Institute in the Chicago area in the early 1970s. That organization is the principal research and education facility for the banking industry in our country.

When Ron assumed management of the institute, it was almost totally dependent upon dues from banks nationwide to finance its operations. When he retired in the late 1990s, it was almost totally dependent upon income-earning functions to finance its operations.

Ron is very bright and industrious, and one of the true visionaries in banking in our country. To convert a national banking organization from reliance on dues for financial support, to one producing products and services commanding fees, is a major achievement. Jim Williams did the same when he was CEO of the Credit Union National Association.

Miami

The Miami Fed is unique for two reasons.

First, it was officially designated as a Federal Reserve branch in the 1970s, the last Fed facility to be so designated. Miami became the twenty-fifth Federal Reserve Branch in our country.

In order to qualify as a Fed branch, Miami had to meet certain criteria, including the required population, the relationship of the number of debits to demand deposits in the region, and the distance from the nearest Fed office.

There are at least two regions that currently meet such criteria for establishment of a Fed branch; the Phoenix area and Hawaii. There no doubt are others. To my knowledge, however, no region has made the kind of effort necessary to be so designated.

The second reason Miami is unique is that it is the only one-story branch building in the entire Fed. It was constructed in Dade County in the late 1970s as an "experiment," according to Phil Coldwell, who was then chairman of the Board's Committee on Federal Reserve Bank Activities and instrumental in the Fed's building program.

The advantages to a one-story building are that Fed operations can be accommodated within with substantial flexibility because of the large amount of contiguous open space, and people and materials do not have to be moved vertically, thus saving on some energy costs.

The disadvantages are that you literally need a golf cart to get from one end of the building to the other, cooling costs are greater because of the loss of the energy advantage of the "layering" of floors found in a multi-story building, and much more acreage is required for the building.

It is doubtful that a one-story Fed branch building will ever be constructed again.

Richmond

The Fourth Fed District's bank building looks like a smaller version of one of the two World Trade Center buildings that were destroyed in the 9/11 terrorist attacks. The reason for the similarities is that the architect for the World Trade Center building, Yamasaki, also was the architect for the Richmond Fed building.

The building was constructed in the 1970s, and much discussion occurred within the Fed prior to the Board's approval of the program. It turned out to be a very fine addition to the Fed's facilities when it was completed.

Bob Black, the first vice president of the Richmond Fed at that time and subsequently its president, marshaled the approval required for this building program through the Board—and not without much consternation. The Board's approval of his appointment as president also was anything but a foregone conclusion. A former Fed governor, among others, was also seeking the position.

Bob ultimately defeated the internal politics, was appointed president, and did a very credible job in the position. He became one of the Fed's "hawks" in the fight against inflationary forces in our economy. I never did understand why some objected to his appointment, but in any case, he proved them wrong.

Denver

The Denver branch was constructed in the 1960s. But shortly after the newly constructed Denver branch of the Federal Reserve Bank of Kansas City was occupied, a problem developed in raising and lowering the huge, heavy steel door leading to the lower level of the building. A concrete ramp led from the street level down to this door, and beyond the door, into the area where armored vehicles would load and unload.

The problem with the door was that on a number of occasions it came crashing down from its open position unexpectedly, and since it weighed tons, this reverberated throughout the building and felt like an earthquake. I was once visiting the Denver branch when this occurred. You definitely knew it happened when it did—the mechanism that was intended to hold it open failed.

Until it could be repaired, it had to be propped open for safety reasons, but nonetheless, it caused anxiety to anyone going up or down that ramp.

It was interesting to observe the drivers of the armored vehicles going under that door as they entered and exited the building. They would stop just before getting to the door, then race the engine, and then virtually peel rubber as they went under the door, with terror in their eyes.

The mechanism eventually was repaired to the relief of all.

Philadelphia

The Third Fed District's bank building was constructed in the late 1960s. Its prominent architectural feature is a "light core" in the middle of the multistoried rectangular building that, in essence, doubles the amount of offices with windows in the building.

Windows are included, of course, as part of the external façade of the building. The hollow middle of the building permitted windows to be constructed in offices facing this light core.

The shape of the building, though permitting additional areas for light to enter the facility, is not the most efficient design to house Fed operations. Contiguous open space is limited on each floor by the shape of the building.

Helena

The Kansas City Fed has a branch in Helena, Montana, and proposed to build a new branch building in the mid-1970s.

The branch manager, and a member of his Board of Directors, scheduled a meeting with us in Washington to "sell" their building program.

Jack Sheehan (who was then chairman of the Board's Committee on Federal Reserve Bank Activities), and I met with them.

Helena is a very small Fed branch, and despite their best efforts to convince us of the need for a new building, we were not impressed and turned them down. The Fed had more pressing matters to deal with, so we suggested some modification to their current facility.

I mention this incident for two reasons. First, the member of the Board of Directors of the Helena branch at this meeting was named "Buck." (I do not recall his last name.) Buck had the largest wrists I have ever seen on a man. He obviously was, physically, a very powerful man.

Second, this incident highlights the countervailing attitudes that are always present between the Board in Washington and the Boards of Directors of Fed banks and branches.

If you are on a Fed bank or branch board, you are always interested in building a new Fed facility in your community. A Fed building program creates jobs and income for a community, and it enables you to boast—if you are so inclined—at your local country club about what you have done for the community.

The Board in Washington, however, is always obligated to choose the most cost-effective solution to the Fed's space needs.

Oftentimes the two countervailing attitudes are not in synch. (Postscript: Sometime after Jack and I left the Fed, a new branch facility was constructed in Helena.)

Atlanta

A new bank building was constructed in the sixth Fed District and occupied in 2001. The building is interesting for three reasons.

First, some of the architectural features of the board's building in Washington were incorporated into the design of the building. These are evident when you compare both buildings.

Second, the same Georgia marble from the same quarry that was used in constructing the facade of the Board building was used in Atlanta.

Third, the new Atlanta facility has an automated cash-handling system. The vaults are five stories tall and contain cranes suspended from the overhead, which move currency and coin into and out of automated forklifts, which, in turn, move cash into and out of the vaults.

All recently constructed Fed facilities are equipped with such an automated cash handling system.

Chicago

The seventh District totally refurbished its original bank building located in the downtown "loop" area, in the early 1990s. This included construction of an addition, on what previously was a bank parking lot, increasing the size of the building by about 25 percent. The refurbishment included "stepped" atriums, bringing daylight into the building—which previously had very little daylight penetration.

Cleveland

The Cleveland Fed, like New York and Chicago, totally renovated its original building and constructed an addition on what previously was the bank's parking lot.

I haven't been in the facility since it was renovated. The old facility had the most impressive executive-office spaces in the entire Fed system. The carpeting was deep blue and trimmed in white and red, and the office furnishings were wood mahoganies.

Other Fed Construction

In addition to the building programs discussed above, the Fed also constructed new banks in Dallas and St. Louis, and new branches in Cincinnati, Baltimore, Charlotte, Utica, Jacksonville, Birmingham, Omaha, Los Angeles, Houston, Seattle, Louisville, and Little Rock.

Thus, since the 1970s, the Fed has replaced all twelve of its bank facilities via new construction or total renovation, and fifteen of its twenty-five branches. All costs have been funded by the earnings of Fed banks.

What Happened to Old Fed Buildings?

Whenever the Fed builds a new bank or branch building, it must remain in the old building until the new building is available for occupancy. This is because Fed operations must be continuous without interruption.

The Fed maintains its buildings in tiptop shape. Old Fed buildings are sold, and these are always in good condition (with the exception of the Minneapolis building, vintage 1960s). Usually, the buildings are converted to serve other purposes. For example, the old Boston Fed building was converted to a hotel.

9

S&L Debacle

The Savings and Loan (S&L) debacle began in the late 1970s and ultimately was resolved in the 1990s.

The failure of one-third of the S&Ls in this country, a total of 1,043, cost the taxpayers $124 billion and the S&L industry another $29 billion, for a total of $153 billion according to Carry and Shibat, *FDIC Banking Review,* "The Last of the Savings and Loan Crisis: Truth and Consequences." A lot of good work could have been done in this country, and worldwide, for such a staggering amount of money.

Much has been published about the problems in the S&L industry that led to the debacle—particularly the dishonesty of some managers and the myriad of management problems that materialized. It is evident that the industry was plagued by incompetency in management. But, there are others who should have shared in the responsibility for this taxpayers' nightmare, and conveniently avoided this albatross. Some of those that avoided sharing the responsibility, as a matter of fact, have been lauded in the press, and till this day they are treated with deference.

Moreover, the Fed did not perform with distinction in fulfilling the roles assigned to it by Congress in dealing with this debacle.

The information I will present below has not been published previously. I will note how widely the responsibility for this scandal extended into our nation's legislative and financial regulatory sectors. Moreover, you will see how and why this taxpayers' nightmare occurred.

The Catalyst

The catalyst for the S&L debacle was the proliferation of money market mutual funds (money funds) in this country that occurred in the late 1970s and 1980s.

The pooling of money for investment purposes was not a new concept. It started in Europe in the mid-1800s, and made its way across the Atlantic to our country in 1893. But up until February, 1970, the pooling of money for investment purposes in the U.S. was primarily for the purchase of stocks and bonds. In February 1970, the first money fund was chartered by the Reserve Management Company, Inc. as "The Reserve Fund," the fund that "broke the dollar" in 2008 because of investments in Lehman. Today, more than $2 trillion is invested in such funds, among a total of over $7 trillion invested in 10,000 stock, bond, and money funds by 83 million investors, as reported by the Investment Company Institute in its *Mutual Fund Fact Book* (2000).

Money funds became popular and flourished in the late 1970s and 1980s. For a good part of this time, I was at the Board in Washington and in a very good position to observe the rise in the popularity of this new financial invention as an investment vehicle.

Regulated Deposit Accounts

Many may not recall that in the 1970s and early 1980s, and prior to that time, the regulators of depository institutions set the interest rates that banks, S&Ls, mutual savings banks, and credit unions could pay to consumers on their deposit accounts—including savings, time, certificates of deposit, and comparable instruments.

Thus, for example, the Fed would set these rates for commercial banks that were members of the Federal Reserve System, while the Federal Home Loan Bank Board (FHLBB) would set these rates for S&Ls and mutual savings banks, and the National Credit Union Administration (NCUA) would set these rates for credit unions.

In essence, consumer deposit rates in financial institutions in our country were "regulated." And, of course, the regulators set these rates at a level that would not create problems for the financial institutions, and which would enable them to enjoy a profit.

Reasons for Money Funds Popularity

These funds flourished in the late 1970s and 1980s because the interest rates that they could pay to consumers were not limited by regulation, and because their financial structure made it possible for them to pay a higher interest rate than depository institutions. As the premium increased between what a consumer could earn on his investments in a money fund versus what he could earn on his deposits in a financial institution, the popularity of the former grew rapidly.

Many such funds were chartered in the 1970s and throughout the 1980s. Consumers were benefiting from the higher interest rates that they were able to pay, and were flocking to them. Some financial institutions began to experience disintermediation problems as consumers withdrew their deposits and moved them to money funds.

Just how did the structure of the balance sheet of money funds enable them to pay the consumer a higher interest rate than a financial institution?

The assets of the funds were short-term investments in money market instruments with maturities of 120 days or less, with the great majority having maturities of 30 days or less. These included Fed funds, short-term time deposits, short-term Fed funds, "Yankees" (a deposit in a branch of a foreign bank operating in the United States), and "Eurodollars" (a dollar-denominated deposit in a foreign bank).

Their liabilities were the investments that consumers placed with them.

This balance sheet structure enabled them to invest money at the prevailing market rate, minus a small amount for their expenses and profits. As their assets matured, they reinvested at the going market rate by rolling over the investments. In a rising interest-rate environment, which is what we had at the time, every time they rolled over their investments, they earned a higher rate of return and were able to pass this along to the consumer.

Financial institutions' assets, on the other hand, consisted of loans that they had made to businesses and consumers.

Banks' assets were primarily commercial loans; S&L assets were residential mortgages; and credit union assets were consumer loans to their members.

Financial institutions' liabilities were the deposits that consumers, and in the case of banks, that businesses as well, placed with them. (Credit unions do not refer to them as "deposits," but rather as "shares.")

Unlike money funds, the assets of financial institutions were not short-term money market investments at prevailing interest rates, but rather, a portfolio of loans that had been acquired over time, in different interest-rate environments that had less-than-prevailing rates.

For example, the aggregate earnings on an S&L's residential mortgage loan portfolio might have been 6 percent. Most of these loans were made years previously, some at 4.0 percent, some at 4.5 percent, some at 5.0 percent, etc.

Moreover, these mortgage loans had 30-year maturities, and thus would take a long time to pay off. Unlike a money fund, which invested all of its assets in short-term money market instruments and, therefore, could benefit from rising interest rates, an S&L was "stuck" with the earnings from its residential mortgage loan portfolio, just like a bank was "stuck" with the earnings from its commercial loan portfolio, and a credit union was "stuck" with the earnings from its consumer loan portfolio.

When interest rates rose, as they did in the late 1970s and throughout the first half of the 1980s as Volcker and the FOMC focused on driving up interest rates to extinguish the fires of rampant inflation, financial institutions were at a significant competitive disadvantage versus the new kid on the block, the money fund. They had to rely on loan portfolio earnings to pay their depositors, and such earnings were at less-than prevailing market rates. Financial institutions just could not pay their depositors the same amount of interest that a money fund was paying to its investors.

And because residential mortgages matured in 30 years, whereas commercial and consumer loan portfolios had substantially shorter maturities, the S&Ls were in the worst competitive position of all of the financial depository institutions.

Banks and credit union loan portfolios would pay off much sooner than those of the S&Ls, enabling them to reinvest the cash flow emanating from paydowns at prevailing market rates a lot faster than S&Ls were able to do.

Financial Institutions Reaction to Money Funds

Initially, the reaction of financial institutions to the proliferation of money funds was to emphasize to the consumer that investments in a fund were not "insured." Unlike a deposit account in a financial institution that was "insured" and implicitly backed by the full faith and credit of the U.S. government, a consumer had to rely upon the management of the fund to do its job well. If it didn't, the consumer could conceivably lose at least part of his investment in the fund.

Of course, the money fund industry recognized early on that the one thing it could not allow to happen was for a consumer to suffer a loss of principal on his investment in a fund. That would be like throwing a wrench into the crankcase. So, the industry took whatever actions that were necessary, including financially supporting funds that had problems, to ensure that the par value of every share in a money fund remained at $1. And till this day, that par value of $1 has been retained by the money funds, except for The Reserve Fund.

As a consequence, although financial institutions vigorously attempted to dissuade consumers from investing in funds because of the "uninsured" nature of the investment, consumers all but ignored the perceived threat and money funds flourished. The consumer decided that earning substantially more on his investment in a fund—at times in excess of 5 percent more than what he could earn in a deposit account in a financial institution—was worth whatever risk was attendant with the investment.

Appeal for Help

As the threat of disintermediation intensified, financial institutions came to Washington, D.C., to plead their case. Without sufficient consumer deposits, ultimately they would be forced to borrow money at prevailing market rates to fund their assets, or to dispose of their loan portfolios at a loss so that the proceeds could be reinvested at market rates. These actions would create losses, and many financial institutions, particularly S&Ls, were thinly capitalized and would be unable to weather the storm.

They came en masse to the nation's capital and proposed—to the legislators, regulators, and the presidential administration—that money funds as they were be regulated.

From the perspective of the bureaucrats in Washington, however, regulation of money funds would be an anti-consumer move, and they were not going to do anything harmful to the consumer.

I spoke to Mitchell about this matter at the time, and he stated, "They [the financial institutions] are not going to get what they want. Taking away the yield premium that consumers are enjoying in these money funds would be an anti-consumer move on our part. We are just not going to do it."

The consumer was benefiting from the higher interest rate on his investment in a money fund, and Washington bureaucrats were not going to risk taking this away from the consumer. Legislators and the administration had to rely upon the consumer's vote to retain office, and the regulators did not want to be considered anti-consumer in any of their regulatory functions, regarding financial institutions.

The Smoking Gun

The solution to the disintermediation threat that surfaced in the nation's capital was a proposal to "deregulate" interest rates that financial institutions could pay to consumers on their deposits. (Credit unions refer to the interest rate that they pay to their depositors [shareholders] as a "dividend rate." In essence, it is an interest rate and treated so for tax purposes by the Internal Revenue Service.)

The Fed, as well as the other financial depository institution regulators, were asked to provide their input to the legislators on this proposal. I had a hand in drafting some of the Fed comments. Miller was Fed chairman and Mitchell, acting as a consultant to the Board, also participated in drafting these comments.

The Fed very distinctly, and emphatically, brought to the legislators' attention the differences in the balance sheet structure of money funds and financial institutions, and also, the differences in maturities of their loan portfolios. The other Federal depository regulators did likewise, including the Federal Deposit Insurance Corporation, the Federal Home Loan Bank Board, the Federal Savings and Loan Insurance Corporation, the Comptroller of the Currency, and the National Credit Union Administration.

Special attention was focused on the S&Ls because of the long-term maturities of their residential mortgage loan portfolios. The problems that they would face in moving to a deregulated environment were accurately forecasted, and the necessity for a long-term transition period to accommodate their special needs was emphasized.

Volcker's Role

What followed was the passage of the Depository Institutions Deregulation Act of 1980, which was voted on and approved by the Senate on November 1, 1979, by a vote of 76–9, and by the House of Representatives on March 27, 1980, by a vote of 380–13.

This act provided for the "orderly phase-out and the ultimate elimination of the limitations on the maximum amounts of interest and dividends which may be paid on deposits and accounts by depository institutions . . . ." It organized and empowered the Depository Institutions Deregulation Committee to do so within a six-year period as soon as feasible, with "due regard for the safety and soundness of depository institutions."

The Deregulation Committee consisted of "the Secretary of the Treasury, the Chairman of the Board of Governors of the Federal Reserve System, the Chairman of the Board of Directors of the Federal Deposit Insurance Corporation, the Chairman of the Federal Home Loan Bank Board, and the Chairman of the National Credit Union Administration Board, who shall be voting members, and the Comptroller of the Currency, who shall be a nonvoting member . . ." (The Fed chairman who served on this committee was Volcker.)

This legislation doomed the S&L industry. It, and primarily the speed with which the Deregulation Committee eliminated regulation of interest rates on deposit accounts in financial institutions, did not provide adequate time for the S&Ls to transition to a deregulated environment. The only way that this legislation could have worked is if interest rates had fallen rapidly, and substantially, in the ensuing years. Just the opposite happened—rates significantly ratcheted upward throughout the first half of the 1980s in Volcker's (he had replaced Miller) and the Fed's unprecedented all out war against inflation.

Of course, the S&L industry was highly critical of Volcker and the Fed. They desired—actually, they required for survival—lower interest rates, and rapidly lower. But the battle being waged by Volcker involved considerably more than survival of the S&L industry. The very survival of our economy was at stake, a far greater threat that did not permit easing of interest rates to accommodate the S&L industry.

The Deregulation Committee, like the S&L industry, was dealt a losing hand by the legislators. The committee was assigned a task in the Deregulation Act that could not be done within the time period specified in the legislation—absent favorable downward movement in interest rates. Unless this occurred, there was no way that the committee could govern and oversee the transition to a deregulated environment by the S&Ls without seriously impeding the safety and soundness of the industry. The committee members understood this, as did the legislators.

Moreover, financial institutions were in Washington, D.C., pleading for deregulation of deposit accounts to be accelerated by the Deregulation Committee to stop the disintermediation that was occurring. It was a case of either paying what the money funds were paying the consumer, or losing the deposits and suffer the consequences.

The legislation was very specific about what each member of the committee had to report, annually, to the Congress during the transition period about the economic viability of depository institutions. (The italics below are mine and are not included in the Deregulation Act text.)

"1. an assessment of whether the removal of any differential between the rates payable on deposit accounts by banks and those by thrift institutions *will adversely affect* the housing finance market or *the viability of the thrift industry:*

174

2. *recommendations* for measures which would encourage savings, provide for the equitable treatment of small savers, and *ensure a steady and adequate flow of funds to thrift institutions* and the housing market;
3. *findings concerning disintermediation of savings deposits from insured banks and insured thrift institutions to uninsured money market innovations paying market rates to savers;* and
4. *recommendations for such legislative and administrative actions as the member involved considers necessary to maintain the economic viability of depository institutions.*"

It is evident that the legislators did not expect "smooth sailing" to a deregulated environment, and were hopeful that the Deregulation Committee could perform some magic.

Smoking Gun #2

On May 20, 1982, the House of Representatives approved the Garn–St. Germain Depository Institutions Act by a vote of 272–91. This legislation, among other matters, authorized S&Ls to directly invest in real estate, including making commercial loans, and allowed the Federal Home Loan Bank Board to alter the way in which S&Ls reported on their regulatory capital requirements.

Now, here was an industry that had done nothing other than make residential mortgage loans since its inception. The typical residential mortgage was $100,000, or less. Suddenly, the industry was empowered to make commercial loans, which is an entirely different type of lending. Moreover, commercial loans are orders of magnitude greater in amount per loan than residential mortgages, millions of dollars instead of a hundred thousand, or less.

S&Ls knew how to make residential mortgage loans. They had been making such loans for years. But they knew nothing about commercial lending. No one in the S&L industry could even recognize a good commercial lender if he or she walked into one's office, applying for a job. This was a recipe for disaster. By the stroke of a legislative pen, the amount of risk that an S&L could undertake, beginning on May 21, 1982, was increased dramatically.

But let's review some of the background information to ascertain why the legislators would permit this type of lending, and the assumption of far greater risk by S&Ls than those to which they were accustomed.

S&Ls lobbied heavily for commercial lending authority with the legislators and regulators in Washington, D.C. Their rationale was straightforward: "Permit us to make commercial loans so that we can benefit from (1) increased origination fees and (2) increased lending rates."

When a borrower seeks a residential mortgage, he usually pays the lender an origination fee to make the loan. Borrowers pay lenders origination fees for commercial loans, but such fees are much higher in the dollar amount than they are for residential loans. Moreover, the interest rate for commercial loans also is higher than it is for residential mortgages.

By 1982, many S&Ls were out of capital, interest rates were ratcheting upward, and the industry was in dire need.

The fund that insured consumer deposits in an S&L, the FSLIC (Federal Savings and Loan Insurance Corporation), had less than $30 billion in its coffers. This amount was not sufficient to close those S&Ls that had run out of capital, and to pay off their insured depositors. Estimates at the time were that in excess of $50 billion would be required to do so. This meant that the taxpayer would have to provide the shortfall, and legislators were not anxious to drop that liability upon their constituents. Instead, they were hopeful that allowing S&Ls to make commercial loans would buy additional time, and somehow salvage at least some of those institutions that were insolvent.

The Federal Home Loan Bank Board also was authorized by the legislation to change the way in which an S&L reported its regulatory net worth, thus enabling the S&Ls that had no capital under the GAAP (General Accepted Accounting Principles) to remain solvent under the RAP (Regulatory Accounting Principles). This, it was generally believed in the industry, would enable such troubled S&Ls to maintain a somewhat positive image while buying some time for a miracle to occur.

The legislators and thrift regulators were running out of options, and these two—commercial lending and RAP capital—were all that was left.

Neither one of these turned out to be a very good idea. And you did not have to be a rocket scientist to anticipate that these two options were going to cause "armageddon" in the S&L industry.

Commercial Lending

People with commercial lending backgrounds that were not successful in the banking and financial industries soon made their way in droves to S&Ls, and were hired.

And borrowers, seeking financing for commercial ventures, were right behind them. The commercial ventures for which they were seeking financing, however, were not top-of-the-line quality. Banks and other financiers of commercial ventures had siphoned off the "A," the "B," and the top half of the "C" type of projects. What was left was the bottom of the barrel, the lower half of the "C" and the "D" and "E" projects, for which financing could not be obtained from banks and other experienced commercial lenders.

I saw the results of this recipe for disaster—and the best way to convey the gross incompetency of S&Ls in commercial lending is to describe my experience.

About one-half of the assets from failed S&Ls in this country that eventually came under the control and management of the Resolution Trust Corporation (RTC), the organization established by Congress to resolve the S&L crisis, came from the Southwest, mainly Texas and Oklahoma.

I was hired in the mid 1980s to assist an S&L in Oklahoma that was experiencing critical problems. Subsequently, I was involved in chartering a company in Texas that performed asset management and disposition services for the RTC. The combination of these two experiences enabled me to have access to over fifty S&Ls that had failed in Oklahoma and Texas. The common thread throughout all of these failures was incompetency in commercial lending.

The large failures, such as Charles Keating's Lincoln Savings, have drawn the attention of the press, and their problems have been dissected for public consumption—oftentimes causing mass heartburn, including that to former Fed chairman Greenspan. In 1985, while serving as a consultant, he wrote a letter in support of Lincoln Savings that later proved to be quite embarrassing to him.

But a significant amount of the cost to the taxpayer of $124 billion for the S&L mess was as a result of what occurred in Texas and Oklahoma.

For example, in Oklahoma, Frontier Federal in Ponca City, had originated fifty-two commercial loans—each for multimillions of dollars. These loans represented about 30 percent of its assets, approximately $250 million. The loans were originated after 1982, in a period of two to three years. What was unusual about this portfolio is that all fifty-two of the loans were in the "tank" when I arrived there in late 1986. Of course, these loans, and the foreclosed properties now owned by the S&L, were among the assets that I focused upon. The chairman and former CEO of the S&L was still there, as was the president. But not for long.

After reviewing the assets in the problem portfolio, I repeatedly called the former CEO into my office to see if perhaps I was missing something—because everything I reviewed would lead a rational individual to wonder how anyone would be stupid enough to make this loan. Our conversations went like this.

"Why in the world did you make these loans of $6.5 million to construct a horse racing track in Wyoming, on a ranch? Wyoming doesn't have a large population. Moreover, the closest large city is Salt Lake City which is two and one-half hours away by car, and populated by Mormons who don't drink or gamble. Who did you expect to come to this track?"

His answer: "Jim, if you had seen the artist's renderings of that track and how beautiful they were."

Now, I must admit that throughout my life, I have been angered when confronting incompetence and stupidity—but in particular, when the perpetrator has been someone entrusted with a responsibility who, by virtue of the position he had, would be expected to know better.

So after I asked him, 'What did that have to do with making this loan?" he retreated, as he often did, to telling me, "I just didn't know what I was doing."

This horse racing track ultimately was foreclosed upon and sold for $300,000. (It couldn't get a cash flow or turn a profit even at that price.) The S&L wrote off $6.2 million.

The former CEO had an interesting story. His father was a founder of the S&L, and upon his father's retirement, he became chairman and CEO.

When gathering background information as to what was going on in the S&L during the time these commercial loans were made, I was told that he had made various trips around the country, apparently to determine what other S&Ls were doing that had similar financial pressures. That did not surprise me because the people in this industry did a lot of that during these trying times. It was an industry full of "copycats."

When he returned from one of these trips to California, he showed up on the eighth floor of the home office, the executive floor, gathered the officers about him, and said, while extending his right hand, with his eyes as big as half dollars, "You see this hand. That hand held John Wayne's gun."

Apparently, a person he visited in California had purchased a gun used by John Wayne in a movie.

I next reviewed eight separate loans made to one borrower—for financing hotels and motels. When I looked into the

179

files, I realized that this lending was a level below incompetency—it was pathetic.

The properties had previously been financed by Vernon S&L and Phoenix S&L of Muskogee, Oklahoma.

Not very much time had transpired between when the S&L made these loans and when they became nonperforming and foreclosure on the properties was required. It was a matter of a few years, and not a decade or more. I mention this because the properties had to be in terrible condition when the S&L agreed to finance them.

The only conclusions I could come to were: (1) the S&L did not perform due diligence on the properties, or (2) it didn't know how to do this, or (3) something else occurred. Those were the only explanations for financing eight category "E" properties as though they were "A" properties.

After foreclosure, the S&L found that one of the properties, a hotel in Massachusetts, had a leaking roof. The ceilings had fallen on the top two floors, and were threatening to do so on the next floor under those. These three floors were "sealed off" with plastic sheeting.

Another of these properties was filled with asbestos.

The S&L ultimately recovered about twenty cents on the dollar on these loans, resulting in a loss of about $14 million.

A $3 million "residual equity note" warranted my attention. After speaking with the counsel who was at the S&L when the note was purchased, I was told that it represented the "residual equity that would remain after a HUD apartment project was sold and the loan paid off.

I said, "You're kidding, right?"

He said, "No."

The S&L also had made a multimillion dollar loan on another HUD project, which I reviewed, and I couldn't understand why it would do so in view of the S&L's financial condition. Under HUD rules, the financing had to be made at a favorable interest rate to the borrower, and there were other material disadvantages associated with such lending. But it did make the loan, and in addition, acquired this "residual equity note" as an investment.

The entire $3 million note was written off by the S&L, and the HUD loan was in arrears and in the "tank," requiring an additional multimillion-dollar write-off.

Every time I looked into a problem commercial loan, I would think, "Well, this one beats them all. These people could not have been thinking when they made this loan." And then I would review the next one, and it set new standards.

The next one was a multimillion dollar loan for which the borrower "paid" the S&L ten origination points, or 10 percent of the loan amount as an origination fee. (Typically, origination points on a reputable commercial loan would be in a range of from one to three points.)

I called the former CEO into my office and said, "Why did you charge the borrower ten points on this loan?" He looked at me, kind of surprised, and said, "We booked the fee as income. We needed it."

I said, "No, you don't understand where I'm coming from. Why didn't you charge the borrower twenty points, or thirty, or fifty? He could not get this property financed anywhere else. That's why he agreed to ten points. He would have agreed to any number you put on the table."

Moreover, the origination fee was incorporated into the loan amount, meaning the S&L lent the borrower the origination points as well as the principal on the loan. The S&L, in essence, booked its own money as fee income. And of course, the appraisal, which the borrower provided, supported the total amount lent, the principal amount, and the origination fee, and showed that such an amount represented 80 percent of the appraised amount of the property. This was intended to "prove" to the S&L that the borrower had 20 percent of his own equity in the property.

As I recall, this loan was in arrears from the get-go. When the S&L was able to foreclose on the loan and had the property appraised, the S&L's appraiser set the value of the property at about 50 percent of the borrower's appraiser's estimate, thus requiring a multimillion-dollar write-off on a loan that had never performed. To temporarily book $500,000 in fee income ultimately cost the S&L in excess of $3 million in losses.

After completing my review of the fifty-two commercial loans that the S&L had made, I called the former CEO into my office and said, "How did you get this done? And in such a short time span. [The S&L was authorized to originate commercial loans in May 1982, and I arrived at the S&L in late 1986.] You made fifty-two commercial loans and they are all in the 'tank.' I could take commercial borrowers' names, place them in a hat, and draw out fifty-two names randomly and I would end up with at least a few loans that performed. You are batting a thousand. You're fifty-two for fifty-two."

He looked me straight in the eye, with a repentant look on his face, and again said me, for about the twentieth time, "Jim, I didn't know what I was doing."

He was trying to convince me that he was stupid—and I wanted to tell him that his effort wasn't necessary. But I suspected there was something else he was not telling me.

He didn't give me any excuses like, "It was a stressful time;" "We were reaching;" "We may have panicked;" "Our staff let us down;" etc. It was always, "Jim. I didn't know what I was doing." That sounded to me like a "cover your ass" answer. You can't be found guilty of stupidity in the court of law.

And then our counsel called me and asked to speak to me privately, in my office. He was doing discovery regarding foreclosure proceedings on the S&L's largest commercial loan—$20 million on a recreational-type project outside the Dallas area.

At the time I had reviewed this loan, I called the former CEO into my office and asked him if he or anyone on the loan committee had read the appraisal on this property prior to approving the loan. His answer was, "I don't recall, but I'm sure staff did." I said, "If you read this appraisal, or if anyone did, you would know that it valued the completed project. You used this value in making the loan, but the project was only about one-third to one-half completed."

Subsequently the S&L had the project appraised at $6 million, and wrote off $14 million.

Counsel came to my office, closed the door, and told me that he had discovered a check—which had cleared—made out to the former CEO in the amount of, as I recall, $50,000, signed by the borrower, with the word "fee" written on it. He also informed me that the president of the S&L had received a sizable amount, $200,000, from the borrower.

I immediately convened a special Board of Directors' meeting, and both the former CEO and the president were terminated for cause. We met with each separately.

In response to the Board's reason for terminating him, the former CEO said it was not a fee, it was something else. As I recall, he said it was a repayment of a loan.

The president said that the borrower had offered to lend him money when the S&L converted from a mutual to a stock S&L so that he could purchase stock. Shortly after accepting the money, he said, he returned it because he had second thoughts.

The board then hired a special counsel to research, investigate, and pursue these matters legally.

Subsequently, before the special counsel had completed its investigation, the Federal Savings and Loan Insurance Corporation (FSLIC) closed the S&L, opened it the next day, renamed it Heartland Federal, and installed new management, including a new board of directors. The financial losses from the commercial loan portfolio could not be overcome, and the S&L was declared insolvent.

FSLIC required the former CEO and the former president to sign an "Order of Prohibition," which prevented either party from ever again participating in the affairs of any federally insured financial institution, or organization affiliated therewith. As a quid pro quo for their signing this document, FSLIC agreed not to pursue legal actions against them. I was told by the regulator that in its view, legal costs would be greater than what could be collected from them—given their resources—if FSLIC were successful in such proceedings.

I was retained by the FSLIC, and agreed to remain until the year's end—during which time I assisted the FSLIC, inserted management with developing the operating plan for the S&L while it was to be under their control, and in managing and preparing the S&L to be sold. I then pursued other interests, including subsequently becoming a contractor for the RTC. In this capacity, I had the opportunity to analyze the assets of about fifty failed S&Ls, primarily in the Southwest.

The quality of these assets were like those of the S&L in Oklahoma, lower C, D, and E properties. After reviewing the loan documents, it was evident that in many cases, the S&Ls ended up with property that had been "flipped" a number of times. We suspected that the eight hotel/motel properties that the S&L in Oklahoma financed (discussed earlier) were "flipped," as our review indicated.

In a flip situation, an inflated appraisal is obtained on a property and financed through an inexperienced and unsuspecting lender, at a level exceeding the market value of the property, and substantially higher than what the seller paid for the property.

The new buyer could be an accomplice, or an inexperienced and unsuspecting buyer who may even be grateful to the seller for arranging financing.

The seller pays off the loan on the property that was financed with the old lender, and pockets the excess proceeds from the new financing. The buyer signs a loan document for the financial institution providing new financing, and is the new owner of the property. The seller has thus "flipped" the property, and the S&L providing the new financing is exposed to a financial loss.

The new buyer may or may not be aware of his exposure, depending upon his naïveté and whether he is an accomplice or not.

Such "flipping" of properties can be repeated a number of times, and in a short time span—depending upon the naïveté of the S&L financing the project. These properties do not have cash flow because of the inflated loan principal, and usually are in arrears early on. The S&L must foreclose and becomes the owner of the property.

It is then that the S&L discovers the true market value of the property—but it is too late. The horse is out of the barn, so to speak. A large write-down of the asset is required, causing a substantial loss for the S&L, and the "legal chase" begins. Although judgments may be obtained against the perpetrators of such "flipping" tactics through legal action, collecting on them is another matter.

For example, we legally pursued a borrower and were successful in obtaining a large court judgment against him. The borrower, at the time, was living in a multimillion-dollar residence in Texas, which he had purchased at just about the time we initiated legal action against him.

He had put all of his assets into the home in an attempt to protect them and avoid exposure to legal action. Texas is a "Homestead Act" state, which means that you cannot take a person's home from him while in pursuit of collecting on a judgment, as well as other legal debts.

We argued in the court that it was obvious from the timing of his actions that he had placed all of his assets into a home because he knew he was liable and that a judgment was going to be rendered against him. We said he did so solely for the purpose of avoiding exposure to the actions of the court.

The judge would not rescind his protection under the Homestead Act. He retained his residence, and we had a large judgment that was going to be difficult to collect.

These types of "borrowers" zeroed in on the Southwest's S&Ls, as evidenced by the composition of their problem asset portfolios. The combination of weak lending staffs, inexperience, and the lack of even fundamental knowledge about commercial lending provided a "playground" for such perpetrators.

And there were other schemes that S&Ls attempted, some in a desperate effort to remain viable.

I recall a huge "boat leasing" portfolio that we valued at 60-80 percent less than what the failed S&L had shown on its books. The scheme was rather simplistic. The S&L would finance a fifteen-year lease on a new boat and, in its computations, would assume a residual value of 75 percent of new costs after the expiration of the lease. This enabled it to show substantial earnings, because the majority of lease payments were booked as interest earnings over the years, and only a small amount was directed toward amortization ("using up" of the asset).

We also found that a "consultant" to the S&L, who apparently dreamed up the scheme and originated the boat leases, was paid $3 million over a few years by the S&L for services rendered.

RAP Capital

Implementation of RAP capital rules delayed the closure of many S&Ls, but it also provided them with an opportunity to increase the depth and width of the hole they had fallen into.

These S&Ls were desperate, and were given a "last chance" to survive. As a result, they attracted deposits by paying high interest rates and utilizing, in many cases, brokerage firms to assist in this effort. As their liabilities grew, so did their assets—with more commercial loans. Thus, the abyss into which they were plunging got deeper and wider.

This second "smoking gun," permitting S&Ls to enter commercial lending with no restrictions attached and to utilize RAP capital, did nothing more than prolong the final day of reckoning—but at a greatly increased cost to the taxpayer.

Placing restrictions on S&L commercial-lending activities—such as "no more than 5 percent of S&L assets could be in the form of commercial loans after one year," and "no more than 10 percent after two years," etc., would have made sense and saved a great deal. But it wasn't done.

Moreover, the legislators' withdrawal in 1986 of Federal tax laws (enacted in 1981) that benefited commercial real-estate investments exacerbated the problem by further decreasing the value of S&L assets.

It is difficult to put a monetary value on how much more was added to the taxpayers' burden in resolving the S&L crisis because of the legislators' decisions authorizing commercial lending and RAP capital, and withdrawing the tax laws benefiting commercial real estate. This number has never been calculated, and probably cannot be today. Based on the composition of failed S&L assets that I looked at, however, it had to be a substantial amount. The taxpayers' burden was, perhaps, 30–40 percent more than it would have been, had the legislators not taken these actions.

Smoking Gun #3

On April 19,1989, the Senate approved the Financial Institution Reform, Recovery and Enforcement Act (FIRREA), by a vote of 91–8, and the House of Representatives approved it by a vote of 314–86. Among other matters, the legislation established the Resolution Trust Corporation (RTC).

This legislation, like that authorizing commercial lending and RAP capital, was not a very good idea.

Staffing the organization was difficult. About 700 employees left the FDIC and joined the RTC, and the remainder of the RTC employees, which totaled over 3,000 nationwide, were "off-the-street" hirings.

Who, among FDIC personnel, would be willing to give up their position and accept a similar one with the RTC that had a limited life of a maximum of seven years? The RTC did not get the "cream of the crop."

Moreover, the difficulty in staffing up with off-the-street personnel in a short time span ensured that quality would be marginal.

And much has been written about the confusing organization of the RTC.

The Board of Directors of the FDIC was also the Board of

the RTC, and William Siedman was chairman of both organizations. Running the FDIC was a full-time job. Running the RTC was a full time-and-a-half job. This structure greatly stretched the FDIC Board.

Greenspan's Role

There was also an RTC Oversight Committee, consisting of the secretary of the Treasury, who was chairman of the committee; the secretary of the Department of HUD (Housing and Urban Development); the chairman of the Federal Reserve Board, who was then Greenspan; and two persons from the private sector. The Oversight Board had its own chief executive and staff.

Under the legislation, this Board was responsible for holding the RTC accountable for its actions. It rarely met as a full Board, and made most of its decisions by shuffling paper around the nation's capital. All of its public-sector members had other substantial responsibilities and, therefore, limited time to devote to this additional duty.

Moreover, the decision-making in the RTC was intentionally set up to require five or more people to approve every decision. Frederick Alt, former RTC Oversight Board senior vice president for finance, said: "It isn't set up to succeed. It's set up to have no one make a move without five people asking why," as cited by Michael Wladman, in *Who Robbed America?* (New York: Random House, 1990, p. 120.).

Thus, getting an answer out of the RTC was difficult and especially so if you were a contractor for them.

And they didn't appear to have a "game plan" when they assumed responsibility for resolving the S&L mess. It sort of evolved, over the years, through trial and error.

For example, I was in the process of marketing a $400 million loan portfolio for the RTC. The person to whom I reported was a young lady in the Dallas office of the RTC with, obviously, little experience.

I told her that we would have to separate the performing loans from the nonperformers, and to market each independently of the other. I explained to her that the purchasers of performing loans were financial institutions, including banks, S&Ls, mutual savings banks, and credit unions, as well as Wall Street organizations.

Whereas, I said, the purchasers of nonperforming loans were the "Household Finance" types of organizations—those with experience in dealing with problem assets.

To maximize the RTC's return on this sale, I stated, would require separate marketing efforts to each of these types of buyers of loans.

She told me that she was not going to allow anyone to "cherry-pick" this $400 million portfolio, and that the nonperforming loans were to be commingled with the performers and sold as one portfolio. We followed her instructions. We had no choice.

Fortunately, we divided the portfolio into two separate $200 million sales, and commingled the performing and nonperforming loans in the first sale.

After due diligence by the potential buyers, their offers came in and all said, essentially, the same thing: "We were going to submit an offer of ninety-six cents on the dollar, but since there were many nonperforming loans in the portfolio, our offer is sixty-two cents on the dollar."

Of course, the actual amount bid by each potential buyer differed, but all stated that they were bidding less because of the presence of nonperforming loans in the portfolio.

I did some calculations on the winning bid. What the winning bidder did was to value the nonperforming loans at zero, and the performing loans at less than market value. I calculated that this commingled strategy cost the RTC about $7 million on the first $200 million portfolio sale.

I went back to the young lady with this evidence, and she quickly changed her instructions to me on the second $200 million portfolio sale. We sold the performing and nonperforming loans separately, and achieved a sales price much closer to market value on each.

At the time, I wondered how many times this mistake was repeated in all of the loan sales that were taking place around the country on behalf of the RTC.

I also thought, "This young lady just cost the RTC $7 million because of her decision, and there is absolutely no accountability for that within the RTC structure."

The "game plan" of the RTC from day one should have been to segregate, as soon as possible, all nonperforming assets from the failed S&Ls. These should have been placed under contract management and sold as early as possible, consistent with achieving a price close to market value.

Deposit bases as well as performing assets should have been "market-to-market" and sold immediately.

The buyers (financial depository institutions, including banks, healthy S&Ls and mutual savings banks, and credit unions) would competitively bid for such and the winner would receive performing assets on the other side of those deposits. Any shortfall of assets would be made up by an infusion of cash from the RTC.

Instead, in many cases, both the FSLIC and later the RTC (after the FSLIC ran out of money and the RTC assumed management of the S&Ls they had closed) attempted to sell S&Ls "lock, stock, and barrel."

After the closure of a failed S&L, it would be recapitalized and reopened as a going concern, temporarily under the management of the FSLIC and later the RTC. The S&L would be managed and "prepped" for sale by a management team under contract to the FSLIC or the RTC, and then marketed.

The problem with this approach is that it greatly increased the cost of resolution to the taxpayer, and it was an ill-conceived plan from the start.

For example, the S&L in Oklahoma that I was brought in to assist was closed by the FSLIC on September 2, 1988.

Attempts to market the S&L were unsuccessful, for various reasons, and this S&L's case was finally "resolved" by the RTC on October 8, 1993, over five years after it was closed.

How was it resolved?

Essentially in the manner I described earlier as the preferred method of dealing with failed S&Ls. This should have been done years earlier.

What were the additional costs to the taxpayer?

Each and every month it remained open required that the FSLIC—and later the RTC after FSLIC itself became insolvent—insert a huge dollar amount of cash to ensure that the S&L remained solvent. Why?

Because the S&L still had on its books the problem assets that it had on the day it was closed in 1988. In essence these assets had to be funded for five years. They produced hardly any earnings, and this earnings "hole" had to be filled each month so the S&L could remain solvent and operating.

I wondered how many failed S&Ls nationwide required such an earnings hole to be filled each month.

Why was this an ill-conceived plan from the start?

Because even if a buyer could be found to take on all of the assets and liabilities of the S&L, there was a risk that—on down the road—the S&L again would fail. Those problem assets would still be in the asset portfolio of the S&L. And—this is key—the FSLIC and the RTC were required to attempt to get the buyer to pay the greatest amount possible for those assets. If, indeed, they were successful in doing so and the price the buyer agreed to pay for those assets was too high, the "drain" on earnings from such assets could again cause the S&L to fail.

But that wasn't all of the RTC's problems with the S&L in Oklahoma.

The S&L had a large mortgage-loan-servicing portfolio that the RTC failed to protect when interest rates fell in the first half of the 1990s.

The management team that the FSLIC had inserted into the S&L, and which was retained by the RTC, had continued to acquire mortgage-loan-servicing rights, a strategy that I initiated in 1986. It was a good business for the S&L because its servicing costs were among the lowest in the nation.

What is mortgage loan servicing?

Monthly residential mortgage payments from homeowners are mailed to a servicer—in this case, the S&L. These are processed by the servicer on behalf of the investors who have financed these mortgages. The servicer forwards the dollars collected to the investors, records the payment information appropriately, and retains a small portion of the dollars collected as a servicing fee.

When interest rates decrease, residential mortgages are refinanced at a lower rate. Refinancing terminates the existing servicing arrangements, and the fee income, as well as the "servicing rights" on such mortgages. Since refinancing of the underlying mortgages is a constant threat, the sophisticated servicers "hedge" this threat to protect themselves against economic loss.

The preferred hedge is what is known as "principal only strips," or "PO strips." Wall Street creates these by directing the principal payment streams from residential mortgages into a security known as a PO strip. (Likewise, Wall Street directs the interest payment streams from mortgages into "interest only strips," or "IO strips.")

The buyer of PO strips acquires these at a deep discount—for example, at sixty cents on the dollar. The discount is determined by the prevailing residential mortgage rate, and by the estimated life of the underlying mortgages.

So, for example, if the residential mortgage rate is 8 percent, the buyer of the PO strip will receive a cash flow of approximately 8 percent on his investment until such time as the strip is totally paid down.

However, and this is key, if interest rates decrease and the underlying residential mortgages are refinanced, the buyers of the PO strips will receive $1 for every 60 cents invested. Why the extra 40 cents? Because that is the amount of cash flow that was "set aside" by Wall Street in creating the PO strip security—and was intended to provide the investor with an 8 percent return during the estimated life of the underlying mortgages. Since the mortgages "paid off" (i.e., were refinanced), the investor gets the 40 cents plus the 60 cents he invested.

PO strips are an effective hedge because (1) as residential mortgages are refinanced, and the servicing rights on such mortgages terminate—thus causing an economic loss to the servicer; (2) the PO strips that the servicer purchased pays off $1 for every 60 cents invested, thus causing an economic gain to offset the loss.

Wall Street firms have the capability to properly match servicing rights portfolios with the proper PO strips to accomplish that "hedge."

Although management of the S&L recommended such hedging of the mortgage loan-servicing portfolio, the RTC would not approve it.

The RTC would not approve the hedge because PO strips are derivative instruments (i.e., derived from residential mortgages), and many S&Ls in the late 1980s and early 1990s were purchasing PO and IO strips as speculative investments—in the hopes of getting lucky on the direction of interest rates and enjoying a profit. Many of these S&Ls lost substantial amounts on such investments.

No one with good sense should purchase these strips as an investment. But as a hedge instrument, these are worthwhile. Greenspan once mentioned derivatives as serving a very useful purpose as hedge instruments. Unfortunately, the RTC in the 1990s did not understand this.

As a result, the S&L lost a substantial amount of its investment in mortgage loan-servicing rights while under RTC management and control. And there was no accountability whatsoever for such poor decision-making by the RTC.

There are other instances that could be cited to showing similar patterns in RTC decision-making. As mentioned earlier, I became a contractor for the RTC, and our business with them included provision of asset-management and disposition services. After such contracts were completed, our net profit was 38 percent of all dollars paid to us by the RTC. Someone didn't get it right at the RTC on the front end.

No calculations have ever been made on how much more the S&L crisis cost the taxpayers than it should have—because of the way the RTC was managed and functioned. But it was a sizable amount. What I saw and experienced with them was going on all over the nation.

The initial estimate by the legislators—derived from information provided by the financial depository regulators—for the cost to the taxpayers for the S&L cleanup was $50 billion. The legislators appropriated this amount in 1989 at the time they passed the FIRREA, and established the RTC.

Ultimately, $124 billion of taxpayer dollars was required, and another $29 billion from the S&L industry, for a total of $153 billion.

Other Threats

Could we have other taxpayers' nightmares? Absolutely. We already had one: The subprime mortgage mess (described in chapter 11), which makes the S&L crisis look comparatively small as our government already committed in excess of $10 trillion to that mess.

An area that needs to be closely monitored in our financial structure involves the governmental and pseudo-governmental organizations that have been established to facilitate the financing of housing. The GNMA (Government National Mortgage Association), the FNMA (Federal National Mortgage Association), and the FHLMC (Federal National Mortgage Corporation) all have very substantial potential exposure stemming from the "guarantees" that they provide to the buyers of mortgage-backed securities, among other matters. An aberration in the housing market, for example, such as a major devaluation in housing prices for whatever reason, would tax the reserves that they have established to deal with that which

194

occurred with the subprime problem. Again, because of the "fallout" from such a disaster, which would expand to others in the financial industry, we could not permit a failure of one or more of these behemoths.

Also not to be overlooked as a potential taxpayer bailout candidate is the Pension Benefit Guarantee Corporation (PBGC), a federal agency that insures the pension funds of many of our corporations and pays pension benefits to employees when their corporations abdicate such responsibilities. The PBGC currently is underfunded by about $25 billion, but it estimates that the current under funding of traditional pensions is about $450 billion nationwide, and all of this liability ultimately could be transferred to the PBGC. If this should happen, it could result in a taxpayer bailout that is three times the size of that required for the S&Ls.

And of course, somewhere out there is the Social Security system . . . .

Bank Mergers and Acquisitions

Many commercial banks have become "too large to fail." If problems developed necessitating taxpayer support to prevent such failures, we would have no choice but to provide financial support—as we did with TARP funds in the subprime case. The alternative would be a collapse of our financial system, and we could not permit this to happen. One large banking failure could bring down hundreds, or even thousands, of our financial institutions. Moreover, the cost to the taxpayer of resolving such a problem could be orders of magnitude greater than that required for the S&L cleanup.

Former Fed Chairman Greenspan was very vocal in appraising the potential for disaster among the GNMA, the FNMA, and the FHLMC in his congressional testimony near the end of his tenure. Among other matters, he advised that because of widespread use of derivatives that are employed by these organizations in attempting to manage their interest rate exposure, a miscalculation by them—if severe enough—could result in catastrophic results, especially when considering the enormous size to which these organizations have evolved. He advised further that these organizations could shrink in size considerably and thus reduce their potential for catastrophe, since there are others in the financial industry who could replicate their functions, including banks. I was very surprised that he testified on such matters in the manner that he did, for two reasons.

First, the Fed has approved all of the bank holding companies that have created our megabanks, and such actions have exacerbated the "too big to fail" syndrome in our banking industry. And many of these were approved on Greenspan's watch. At year's end, 2004, only 355 of the large, top-tier bank holding companies (those with assets over $1 billion), out of a total of 5,151 top-tier bank holding companies, held 87 percent of all commercial bank assets in our nation. It is difficult to believe that one of the original purposes of the Federal Reserve Act was to prevent the pyramiding and concentration of bank assets that had contributed to bank failures during the nineteenth century and the beginning of the twentieth. We have come 180° since then, and bank assets are again substantially concentrated.

Second, the banks that these holding companies control employ derivatives extensively in attempting to manage their interest-rate exposure, just as GNMA, FNMA, and FHLMC does. The same warnings that Greenspan voiced concerning these organizations applied as well to these banks, and he was the Fed chairman and regulator of such banks.

10

Chairmen Extraordinaire

There have been eight Fed chairmen since our president began designating a person to serve in that capacity in the Federal Reserve System. Marriner Eccles was the first, and he served from 1934 to 1948; Thomas McCabe was the second, from 1948 to 1951; William McChesney Martin was the third, from 1951 to 1970; Arthur Burns was the fourth, from 1970 to 1978; G. William Miller was the fifth, from 1978 to 1979; Paul Volcker was the sixth, from 1979 to 1987; Alan Greenspan was the seventh, from 1987 to 2006; And Ben Bernanke is the eighth, taking over the Fed's gavel on February 1, 2006.

I worked with three of these men, Burns, Miller, and Volcker.

Arthur Burns

Burns was the most intelligent person that I ever had the privilege of meeting, working with, and observing, both in business and social settings.

He also had a "presence," for the lack of a better descriptive word, that would turn heads when he walked into a room. His full head of white hair, parted in the middle, with his dark conservative business suit, and his ever-present pipe, conveyed a very professional and dignified image.

It never failed to amaze me that when he walked into a business or social setting, you sensed that everyone in the room was aware that he had arrived, much like you would expect the reaction to be if our president entered the room.

These two characteristics, his superior intellect and commanding presence, served him well as the "chief executive officer" of the Fed. He was respected by all within the Fed, and there were very few, if any, who would seriously challenge him. And those that did so did it very carefully.

Many Fed people, and others outside the Fed, were intellectually intimidated by him. And not because he was an intellectual bully, but rather, because they were aware of his brainpower and ability to use it.

Everyone in the Fed addressed him as "Mr. chairman" at all times—except for Mitchell, who always called him "Arthur." They were both about the same age, and perhaps that had something to do with it.

There are two incidents, among many others, that come to mind, that convey the power of Burns as the leader of the Fed.

The first occurred in the early 1970s when Ron Burke (who was then director of the Division of Federal Reserve Bank Operations) and I entered a Board member's outer office. His secretary was sitting at her desk, and Ron noticed a "buzzer"-type button on the desk, which he pushed down with his thumb, while asking the secretary, "What's this for?"

She responded, "Oh, you shouldn't have done that."

And just about the time the last word came from her mouth, the door to the Board member's office burst open—and there stood the Board member, still in the process of buttoning his pants.

The secretary said, "I'm sorry, Governor, but Mr. Burke accidentally pushed the buzzer."

The Board member looked at us, expressionless, and retreated into his office, closing the door behind him.

Burke then asked the secretary, "What the hell was that all about?"

She explained that the Board member "had a buzzer installed in his 'john,' and if the chairman calls while he is in there, I am to buzz him."

Name me another chairman, inside or outside the Fed, who commanded that type of attention.

The second incident also occurred in the 1970s.

The Board's Committee on Federal Reserve Bank Activities and its support staff had met with the presidents of all the Federal Reserve banks, and their staffs, in formulating the Fed's budget for 1975. Of course, much staff work precedes such meetings.

After these meetings take place, the adjustments agreed upon are made to each Fed Reserve bank's budget, and these are aggregated along with the budget for the Board of Governors and its staff. This becomes the proposed Fed budget for the coming year, which must then be approved by the full Board.

The budget that was put forth to the Board, for its final approval, called for an increase of 19 percent over the previous year's expenditures.

The presidents of the Fed Reserve banks had all come to Headquarters in Washington, forcefully pleading their case for substantial increases in their budgets. They all stated that it was time to "catch up" on the "deferred" items that were removed from the previous three years' budgets at the direction of the Board.

An afternoon meeting was scheduled for Board review of the budget, and in this case, the Board members were going to see the budget for the first time when they took their seats at the Board table. Various delays in assembling the budget precluded providing it to the Board members in advance of the meeting.

Staff occupied the Boardroom early in preparation for the meeting, and eventually, the Board members took their seats at the appointed hour.

Chairman Burns looked at the very top page of the budget proposal, saw the 19 percent proposed increase in expenditures, and exploded.

The meeting lasted less than ten minutes. Burns told everyone in the room, including Board members and staff, that there was no way he was going to go to the Hill and to the White House with such an increase. He stated that he had been lecturing—for a considerable period of time—Congress and the Administration on the need to curtail government expenditures and to bring down the deficit. (Arthur Burns taught his students, while he was a professor at Columbia, that the main cause of inflation was excessive government spending.) This level of increase, he said, would make the Fed look foolish.

He then abruptly got up from his seat at the Board table and left the room. The meeting was over.

The presidents of Fed Reserve banks again were called to Headquarters, given the facts of the situation, and their budgets were drastically reduced. The "revised" Fed budget called for an increase of 5.9 percent over the previous year's expenditures. And everyone in the entire Fed system bought into that budget.

That was the epitome of CEO power in action. It is doubtful that any other Fed chairman could have done the same. It reminds me of a similar situation that I came across in another industry that you may find interesting.

A good friend of mine for over forty years, Don Lawrence, is a retired NFL football coach. When we met in Washington, D.C., in the early 1960s, he had just been cut as a defensive tackle from the Washington Redskins, and he decided to pursue a career in coaching.

Among other achievements, Don went to four Super Bowls with the Buffalo Bills. I asked him what made Buffalo's Marv Levy such a successful head coach, and I told him not to give me a laundry list, but the one thing that stood out.

He thought a minute and told me that "Marv is an outstanding leader."

I asked him what that really meant.

He stated that "Marv could get the players to 'buy' into what he was advocating, and, he was able to keep the players' confidence. If you can't do that, you can't be successful as a coach in the NFL."

It occurred to me that you cannot be successful as Fed chairman unless you can do likewise.

And Burns did not just have credibility with Fed people. The legislators, both House members and senators, had great respect for him.

Burns, unlike other Fed chairmen, including Greenspan, went to testify on the Hill by himself. No one accompanied him. In the evenings, I would watch replays of such testimony on TV.

Those legislators reminded me of "students" at the feet of the professor. It was obvious that they were attentive to every word that he uttered—and they shook their heads in agreement with most points that he made.

On occasion, a question would be addressed to him that caused me to think, "Congressional staff really researched that thoroughly. That is one hell of a tough question. I'm not sure how I would answer that."

And Burns would proceed to fiddle with his pipe, and perhaps, even light it—in order to buy some time before answering.

Then he gave his answer—and I would think, "Terrific. I wish I had thought of that."

Well, I wasn't the only one watching that testimony. So was the entire Fed system.

Burns could enjoy humor, even when he was the brunt of it, which only happened once.

At George Mitchell's retirement luncheon in the Martin Building, a kind of "roast" was planned and I, among others, was asked to say something—preferably humorous. In attendance would be all of the Board members, Fed Reserve bank presidents, first vice presidents and the staff, and the Board's staff.

After food was consumed, the "roast" began. Eventually, the mike was brought to me, and I said: "Everyone in this room knows that I worked closely with Governor Mitchell on payments-mechanism matters. But some of you don't know what kind of pressure that entailed."

I remember telling Governor Mitchell that we could not put another RCPC on the consent calendar because of the costs involved. But he said to me, "Don't worry about the costs, Jim, the chairman will be out of town."

All in the room were aware of Burns's insistence that anything requiring the expenditure of dollars could not go on the consent calendar. And all were aware of his position, that "we are the custodians of the public purse."

Therefore, my comment brought down the house. And Burns, standing on the podium with Mitchell, was laughing as hard as I had seen him laugh—and pointing and shaking his index finger at me in mock chastisement.

After the meeting, Willis Winn, president of the Cleveland Fed, said, "Jim, yours was the best"—and he was still laughing.

Burns was as compassionate a man as there was in the Fed. He always referred to Fed people as "Fed family," and treated them accordingly.

For example, when the general counsel of the Board, Tom O'Connell, saw his diabetes worsen and cause him to give up the position, Burns established a new position at the Board, "counsel to the chairman," and Tom remained in the same office, at the same pay, until his demise.

Tom was a great banking attorney, one whom Burns, and the entire Fed system, relied upon—especially when the legal issues became complex. And even though he was handicapped at the very end by the seriousness of his condition, he continued to provide outstanding counsel on the matters he was able to handle, which included providing legal advice to Mitchell and me on our Fed-related work.

Jerry Hawke, another outstanding attorney, replaced him as general counsel and the two worked very effectively together—just what you would expect, given the quality of the two.

Burns also is unique among Fed chairmen for the number of Fed people that were appointed to the Board during his tenure.

Some Fed chairmen are more influential than others in

presidential appointments to the Board. Bob Holland and Chuck Partee, from the Board staff, and Phil Coldwell, former president of the Dallas Fed, were appointed to the Board while Burns was Fed chairman. It is not a common occurrence for our president to appoint Fed people to the Board. Burns's influence in this regard is an exception. For example, the previous Fed chairman, Greenspan, attempted to get Ted Turner, director of the International Division, appointed to the Board, and the then President Clinton refused to do so. Greenspan was, however, later successful in getting Donald Kohn, the staff research director, appointed to the Board.

The entire Fed system was aware of Burns's support of Fed people for presidential appointments to the Board, and his success in getting them appointed—and this increased their "awe" of him.

I recall a similar incident of a leader supporting those under him, but in an entirely different situation.

In May 1960, I was an officer on board the USS *Tidewater* (AD-31), a destroyer tender on a Mediterranean cruise. We were docked in Naples, Italy, and the Greek royal yacht was tied up directly behind us. (It was a converted military craft and still looked as such.) All from the Greek Royal Family, except the king, were aboard the yacht.

Captain William A. Hunt, Jr., and Commander W.F. Toy, our commanding officer and executive officer, decided to invite the royal family aboard our ship for a steak dinner and a movie, and they accepted.

Shortly after the invitation was extended and accepted, I heard them discussing the matter, and their decision to await informing the Navy and the State Department of the Greek royal family's visit until after it had occurred. If they did so in advance of the visit, they stated, our ship would be full of diplomats and the ship's officers would be excluded.

So, that evening, Queen Frederica of Greece, her son, Crown Prince Constantine (now the king), Princess Sofia (now the queen of Spain and married to King Juan Carlos), and Princess Irene came aboard and had dinner with us in the wardroom—and stayed for two movies. (Queen Frederica explained that her husband, King Paul, was engaged in state business in Athens.) They were very charming, gracious, good-looking, and not at all pretentious. We had a marvelous evening.

(At the 1960 Rome Olympics, Prince Constantine won a gold medal as a member of the Greek sailing team, and his sister, Princess Sofia, was a reserve on the team.)

The following morning, after reporting the visit to the authorities, Captain Hunt received a scathing message—indicating that he should have informed the Navy and the State Department before the visit so that proper protocol and procedures could have been followed.

Word got around the ship about his concern to ensure that his officers participated in the event, and that it "cost" him with the Navy. We did our best to make it up to him.

The Burns Rumor

There are some who have questioned Burns's performance as Fed chairman.

Martin, a writer referred to earlier, states in his book, *Greenspan: The Man Behind the Money,* that "Arthur Burns . . . could never quite shake the rumor that he had caved in to Nixon during the 1972 election year and provided easy money" (p. 168).

Jones, a Ph.D. economist, goes even further and states in his book, *Unlocking the Secrets of the Fed,* that Burns "suffered from an excessively cozy political association with the Nixon administration . . ." (p. 184).

I was inside the Fed for a considerable period of time, and therefore, can enlighten you as to the "roots" of rumors such as this.

Whenever a Fed chairman gets called to the White House, speculation begins among Fed staff, and even Board members, as to the underlying reasons. Of course, whatever is going on at the time in our country that can be related to the reason for the meeting is part of the speculation. If we are nearing a presidential election, then the "grapevine" begins to connect the chairman's visit to the White House with a presidential request "to keep interest rates low until after the election."

No one in the Fed, except the chairman himself, is privy to what is discussed at these meetings. Sometimes the chairman will subsequently divulge a portion or more of what was discussed, and, at other times, will say nothing about the meeting.

Moreover, the Fed system has the most efficient "grapevine" in the world. I have, on occasion, told a person in a Fed Bank unusual information in the morning, and had it repeated to me by a person in another Fed Bank on the opposite side of our country that same afternoon.

Writers rely upon their sources for what they report, and will seek to corroborate what they are told—that is, receive the same information from more than one source.

Trust me. You can find corroboration among two or three Fed workers and former Fed personnel, for almost any speculation you wish to make about meetings between the Fed chairmen and our presidents. Sometimes mere corroboration is not sufficient.

I knew Burns and worked with him daily. All of his actions as Fed chairman that I ever observed were the epitome of integrity. Moreover, he demanded as much from those he relied upon for counseling. There was no faster way to lose credibility with him and his confidence in you than to be less than candid, forthright, and honest with him. The importance that he placed upon integrity is illustrated, for example, in his message on a photograph that he personalized for me at my request. He wrote, "With warm admiration of your scholarship and your personal character."

Burns was just not capable of abdicating his responsibilities for political expediency and mortgaging his personal integrity. Additionally, in order to buy into Martin's and Jones's innuendoes, you would also have to assume that the other eleven voting members of the FOMC abdicated their responsibilities, as well. That's just not possible.

This "rumor" involving Burns began to be publicly "aired" sometime after his demise. Burns passed away at Johns Hopkins in 1987 at the age of eighty-three, following surgery to remedy a health problem that had materialized when he was ambassador to West Germany. I can think of nothing that would have caused him to intellectually bludgeon a criticizer more than an attack on his personal integrity.

No one inside or outside of our country—not a professional journalist, nor any economist, nor a Fed watcher, nor any banker, nor any businessman—has ever granted to Burns the credit he deserves for modernizing the Fed's, and this nation's, payments mechanism. A large part of this book showed you how that was done. And it all happened on his watch, orchestrated by George Mitchell.

When Miller replaced Burns as Fed chairman in 1978, we had a going-away party for him. We sang, "For he's a jolly good fellow." I think he enjoyed it. Sometime afterward, he was appointed ambassador to West Germany.

Before leaving the Fed, Burns inquired about the cost of retaining a chauffeur. He had never learned to drive, and would no longer have access to a car and a driver after departing. When told of the cost, he dismissed that as an option. He was not a wealthy man.

G. William Miller

Miller served as Fed chairman for seventeen months, after which he became Secretary of the Treasury in 1980 during President Carter's Administration.

Although all addressed him as "Mr. chairman" at Board meetings, he asked me (and others) to call him "Bill," which I did when outside of the Boardroom.

Miller had been a very successful, and a nationally known businessman prior to becoming Fed chairman. In addition to his business background, he also brought to the chairman's position his experiences as a member of the board of directors of the Boston Fed.

Because he was not an "economist" by education or by profession, the economic community from the outset was "cold" toward his appointment as Fed chairman. (Their unspoken position was that lack of a formal education and professional background in economics excluded a person from handling the Fed chairmanship's responsibilities. I often wished I had the opportunity to confront them with the argument that lack of an educational and professional background in presidential matters excludes a person from handling the chief Executive's responsibilities in our country.)

I worked with Miller daily and got to know him as well as anyone in the Fed, and better than most.

To begin with, Miller was not Fed chairman long enough to leave the type of legacy that all of his colleagues left behind. After seventeen months you are just getting "settled in," and suddenly the rug is pulled out from under you.

Miller's appointment as Fed chairman was a "gutsy" move by the then President Carter. He broke with tradition by placing a noneconomist in the job.

I was disappointed when Miller left the Fed, for three reasons.

First, we had an opportunity to see what a businessman could bring to the job—and seventeen months was not enough time to draw any conclusions. Much of what the Fed focuses on in its monetary-policy formulation is business related. Take a look in any Fed district's "beige" book and you will see what I mean. (Periodically, a beige book, which describes the business and economic conditions prevalent in each of the twelve Fed districts, is prepared for the FOMC by each Fed Bank.)

Second, leadership ability is an enormously important ingredient for being a successful Fed chairman. Even the purists among the economists would agree that a successful CEO like Miller got to the pinnacle in the business world because he could lead people.

Third, monetary-policy formulation consists of twelve votes, one of which belongs to the chairman. Moreover, behind those 12 votes are economic research and analysis resources, and advisors, second to none in the world. A Fed chairman does not create monetary policy in a vacuum.

I was especially interested in seeing how Miller would handle the total CEO role that belongs to the Fed chairman, much of which requires business management skills. Until he departed, he was doing an admirable job. That's not just my opinion, but it also was the opinion of George Mitchell—one of the most successful vice chairman the Fed ever had. And who would be better qualified than Mitchell to make this assessment about Miller?

One of the things Miller did, almost immediately upon assuming the job, was to chair Board meetings more efficiently. He believed that the Board could get its job done in substantially less time. The length of Board meetings decreased, and they became much more businesslike.

Miller was one of the best-dressed men in the nation's capital while he was Fed chairman, thanks to his wife. He is color-blind, and she purchased his suits, shirts, ties, socks, and shoes, and selected and matched what he wore each day. (I learned this at a luncheon she organized to surprise him on his birthday. Somehow the subject of clothing came up.)

He was more of a private person than Burns, who preceded him, and Volcker, who followed him. This was apparent in his first day on the job.

Miller saw to it that certain Fed people, including me, were invited to the White House when President Carter officially announced his appointment as Fed chairman.

I arrived at the west gate of the White House, on Pennsylvania Avenue, in a Fed car with others who attended—about two hours before the scheduled ceremony. The security guards at the gate checked off our names on the list of those invited, and we then drove up the incline to the main entrance of the mansion. We were escorted into the White House and deposited one level below that on which the East Room is located—where the ceremony was to take place.

We were then left on our own to "browse" around, after being politely informed of the boundaries that we were to respect. Among the things that I recall from such a once-in-a-lifetime experience was the display of china from previous presidents, including Lincoln. It was fascinating and exciting to be able to explore, on my own, some of the White House. That was one of the quickest two-hour periods I ever experienced.

We were all then escorted to the East Room at the appropriate time. Chairs had been set up facing to the south in the room to focus on an elevated platform on which the ceremony would take place.

After all were seated, we heard "Hail to the Chief" being played, and President Carter entered the room from the same corridor that we did, and we all stood up. He walked up on to the platform and the ceremony began.

When Miller made his brief remarks, he appeared somewhat uncomfortable, as differentiated from being nervous, which he was not—or at least didn't appear to be.

I am not sure he ever became comfortable with the limelight and notoriety that accompany the Fed chairmanship. He was at his best in a businesslike setting as opposed to a formal ceremonial type of atmosphere.

Paul Volcker

Volcker's place in Fed's monetary economic history is etched in stone. He led the Fed through its most challenging period in monetary history since the Great Depression, with courage and single-mindedness, and stamped out—first the fires, and ultimately the remaining embers of inflation—that seriously and dangerously threatened our well-being. He was the right man, in the right place, at the right time. Few would argue that.

The tallest among all of the Fed chairman at 6'7", his "rumpled" appearance and short, inexpensive cigars were his trademark.

He was president of the New York Fed when Carter moved Miller to Treasury in 1979 and appointed him Fed chairman.

While he was president of the New York Fed, I was involved in a number of confrontations between the Board and his bank. One of these, the New York Fed's building program, has already been discussed in chapter 7. It was cancelled by the Board.

The second incident occurred during the Fed budget process.

Paul Volcker and a few members of his staff—including Gerry Corrigan—met with the Board's Committee on Federal Reserve Bank Activities in the Special Library in the Board building. I was present, as well as the key budget staff members in my division.

Phil Coldwell was chairman of the committee, recently having been appointed a Board member. He agreed to give up the Dallas Fed president's job at the request of Burns, and took a considerable cut in pay.

These budget meetings with Fed Reserve banks were contentious. No one, least of all a Fed bank president, enjoys being questioned—and in the president's view, "second guessed"—on proposed expenditures. Moreover, they argued aggressively to preclude the reductions that were made to their budgets as a result of these meetings.

Paul Volcker entered the Special Library with antipathy on that day. He sat across the table from Coldwell. During the entire meeting, he kept his back toward Coldwell—never facing him directly, but instead facing his staff people who were seated behind him, and periodically engaging in conversation with them.

I was at the head of the table so that Coldwell was on my left, and Volcker, on my right.

Volcker proceeded to light one of his trademark short, inexpensive cigars with a match. With his back toward Coldwell, he threw the match in the general direction of the ashtray, which was directly in front of Coldwell. (Coldwell smoked unfiltered Pall Malls, and he always had an ashtray in front of him.)

Volcker overshot the ashtray, and the match landed on the left sleeve of Coldwell's suit jacket, (which he was wearing). And the match was still lit.

Coldwell quickly blew out the match, placed it in the ashtray, and was blowing on, and rubbing, the left sleeve of his suit jacket to extinguish the embers. Phil Jackson, a Board member on the committee, had a stunned look on his face as he observed what occurred. Volcker never turned around to face Coldwell or Jackson.

Now, I can't say that Volcker deliberately threw that match with the intent of having it land on Coldwell. But he did not take actions to ensure that it landed safely in the ashtray—such as blowing it out and placing it there.

I can only guess at what put Volcker into a cantankerous mood that day.

There was a third incident—one in which my division at the Board took a position on an operating matter involving Fedwire that was diametrically opposed to the position taken by the New York Fed on the same issue.

Ultimately, a telephone conference call was arranged with Miller, then Fed chairman, and me on one end of the call, and Volcker and a few of his staff people on the other end. The purpose of the call was to hear each side out—and in so doing, to hopefully get the matter resolved.

After quite a bit of bantering back and forth, Miller finally got Volcker's attention and told him that he "couldn't talk while we were talking," because the equipment would not facilitate a simultaneous two-way conversation. He had to wait until we finished, and we had to do likewise.

The discussion was very testy, and ended as a stalemate. However, the Board decided to accept the recommendation of my division, and that's how the matter was resolved.

On the Friday evening when the TV newscasters reported Miller's move to Treasury and Volcker as President Carter's new Fed chairman, I felt much like Kevin Kearney did when commenting on Shleiminger's Christmas present. I thought, "Oh, shit . . ."

My anxiety was not necessary. When Volcker took the helm at the Fed, neither Coldwell nor I had any reason for concern. In our dealings with Volcker, the past stayed in the past.

In taking the Fed chairmanship, he accepted a job that paid two-thirds less than what he had made as the New York Fed's president—which at that time was the highest-paying job in the Fed. I am very familiar with the Fed's pay scale. Among other matters, the division I directed assessed the performance of the twelve Reserve banks, their presidents, and first vice presidents, and recommended to the Board their annual adjustments in compensation.

Moreover, while his income was cut by two-thirds, his living expenses increased because he had to maintain two residences, one in New York and one in Washington. (His wife was ill at the time and remained in New York.)

The "rumor" at the Board was that he used stacked plastic milk crates for lamp tables in his Washington apartment.

When a banker gave him a box of expensive cigars as a gift, he returned these, stating he might get used to them but couldn't afford them.

Volcker left the Fed in 1987 and joined an investment banking house on Wall Street. Like Burns, he was not a wealthy man when he left the Fed.

Alan Greenspan

Marriner Eccles, William McChesney Martin, and Alan Greenspan had the longest tenures as the Fed chairman—Eccles was chairman for fourteen years; Martin, for nineteen years; and Greenspan, for eighteen years.

You don't remain in the job for that length of time unless you are doing something right. As you know, Greenspan was a very popular and respected chairman, not only in our country, but worldwide. Eccles and Martin were thought of similarly during their time in the job.

Of course, I did not "see" Eccles and Martin perform as Fed Chairman—but I have seen Burns, Miller, Volcker, Greenspan, and now Bernanke for a short period of time. I have often thought about how a meeting between those five would transpire if they were placed together in the Boardroom discussing Fed business. My assessment is that Burns would be the dominant personality, followed closely by Volcker. Greenspan would be the one attempting to arrive at a consensus among the five, and Bernanke would be encouraging everyone "to speak their piece." Miller, on the other hand, would grant to each their opinion, and respect such.

How have each of these contemporary Fed chairmen performed in managing the total Fed? School is still out on Bernanke, and he is the subject of this book's final chapter, but let's consider the other four.

First, let's look at how well they did in meeting their two congressionally mandated objectives in conducting our nation's monetary policy: price stability and full employment. Since our legislators in Washington represent us, these are, in essence, our mandates to the Fed.

Column 1 of Table 1 shows the tenures of Burns, Miller, Volcker, and Greenspan. Burns assumed the Fed chairman's job in 1970, he was replaced by Miller in 1978, who was replaced by Volcker in 1979, and Greenspan replaced him in 1987.

Column 2 of Table 1 shows our nation's rate of inflation each year since 1971. (The Consumer Price Index is the most widely accepted measure of inflation, and thus price stability, that we have.) Column 3 shows our unemployment rate over the same period, the reciprocal of which is the employment rate in our economy. The Fed's job, according to its congressional mandate, is to promote low numbers in these two columns consistent with sustainable growth in the economy. (The Fed does not publicly disclose whether or not it has numeric targets for

Table 1

Chairman	1 Year	2 Rate of Inflation (a)	3 Unemployment Rate (b)	4 Net Fed Expenses (c)	5 Annual Percent Change	6 Annual Percent Change Adjusted for Inflation
Burns	1970			297800		
	1971	4.4	5.9	352242	18.3	13.9
	1972	3.2	5.6	383151	8.8	5.6
	1973	6.3	4.9	461291	20.4	14.1
	1974	11.0	5.6	517352	12.2	1.2
	1975	9.1	8.5	547936	5.8	(3.3)
	1976	5.8	7.7	599957	9.5	3.7
	1977	6.5	7.1	616217	2.7	(3.8)
Miller	1978	7.6	6.1	645880	4.8	(2.8)
Volcker	1979	11.3	5.8	675598	4.6	(6.7)
	1980	13.5	7.1	780264	15.5	2.0
	1981	10.3	7.6	877353	12.4	2.1
	1982	6.2	9.7	987847	12.6	6.4
	1983	3.2	9.6	1095229	10.9	7.7
	1984	4.3	7.5	1184560	82	3.9
	1985	3.6	7.2	1205122	1.7	(1.9)
	1986	1.9	7.0	1254206	4.1	2.2
Greenspan	1987	3.6	6.2	1228781	(2.0)	(5.6)
	1988	4.1	5.5	1290371	5.0	.9
	1989	4.8	5.3	1421741	10.2	5.4
	1990	5.4	5.6	1453478	2.2	(3.2)
	1991	4.2	6.8	1538953	5.9	1.7
	1992	3.0	7.5	1603486	4.2	1.2
	1993	3.0	6.9	1798266	12.2	9.2
	1994	2.6	6.1	1942194	8.0	5.4
	1995	2.8	5.6	1979764	1.9	(.9)
	1996	2.9	5.4	2110503	6.6	3.7
	1997	2.3	4.9	2150860	1.9	(.4)
	1998	1.6	4.5	2011445	(6.5)	(8.1)
	1999	2.2	4.2	2065952	2.7	.5
	2000	3.4	4.0	2159755	4.5	1.1
	2001	2.8	4.7	2379764	10.2	7.4
	2002	1.6	5.8	2432189	2.2	.6
	2003	2.2	6.0	2759678	13.5	11.3
	2004	2.6	5.5	2511036	(9.0)	(11.6)
	2005	3.5	5.1	3155286	25.7	22.2

(a) Annual percent change in Consumer Price Index. Source: U.S. Department of Labor, Bureau of Labor Statistics.

(b) Annual unemployment rate (not seasonally adjusted, sixteen years and over). Source: Bureau of Labor Statistics.

(c) Includes Fed Banks' expenses minus U.S. Treasury reimbursements for Fed services received and Board expenses, in thousands of dollars. Source: 92nd Annual Report, 2005, Board of Governors of the Federal Reserve System.

inflation and unemployment. From time to time, however, these are discussed during FOMC meetings.)

In this regard, zero, or any positive number close to zero, or any negative number in columns 2 and 3 would be undesirable. Such a number in column 2 would create major concerns with disinflation, and in column 3, would result in an inflationary labor market in which employers would competitively bid up wages in their quest to meet employment requirements.

Our rate of inflation surged during Burns's tenure to 11 percent in 1974, and then abated over the following three years. (The 11 percent jump in 1974 is why some have speculated about Burns accommodating President Nixon with low interest rates in the 1973 election year. I have addressed such speculation earlier.)

As Burns increased interest rates to bring down inflation in years subsequent to 1974, you can see the effect of such action on the unemployment rate in column 3, which increased. Higher interest rates slow down economic growth and wring out inflation by making the cost of capital and credit more expensive to business and consumers, thereby reducing investment and consumption. As a result, jobs ultimately are lost in our economy and unemployment increases.

Paul Volcker inherited a surging inflation during the years 1979 to 1986 and dealt with it vigorously. You can see this in columns 2 and 3 of Table 1. Inflation was defeated under Volcker, but the cost was substantial, as shown in column 3. The unemployment rate ratcheted up from 5.8 percent at the start of his tenure, approached 10 percent in the middle, and eased down to 7 percent at the end, still a relatively high number.

Particularly in Volcker's years can you see the delay between the Fed's interest-rate increases and the time necessary for such to work its way through the economy and be fully felt. The peak years of inflation were 1979–1981. And the peak years of unemployment were 1981–1983. The Fed increased interest rates aggressively during this surge in inflation, but the

215

full impact of these on employment was delayed by about two years.

Today, each percentage point in unemployment equates to about 1.507 million people in our labor force, of the 150.7 million being out of work. In June 2006, our unemployment rate was 4.4 percent, resulting in just over 6.63 million seeking jobs. Today, our unemployment rate is approaching 10 percent because of the recession we are experiencing as a result of the effects of the subprime problem.

Under Greenspan, there was some ratcheting up of inflation during the period 1988–1990, and again in 2004 and 2005, the latter attributable to oil and energy price increases, and also growth of unemployment in 1990–1992. But even considering these, the numbers attributed to his Fed chairmanship shown in columns 2 and 3 were remarkable. He achieved a "smooth" array of low numbers, thus avoiding gyrations and perturbations, and a balance between price stability and full employment that has set the standard for all subsequent Fed chairmen.

Now let's look at how well these Fed chairmen performed as "custodians of the public purse."

Column 4 of Table 1 shows annual net Fed expenses since 1970; column 5 shows the annual percentage change in such expenses; and column 6 shows the annual percentage change in such expenses after inflation.

Fed expenses grew from $298 million in 1970, Burns's first year as chairman, to $2.76 billion in 2003, Greenspan's sixteenth year as the Fed leader. During the thirty-four-year period depicted in Table 1, the Fed experienced eleven years of double digit annual increases in expenses—three under Burns, four under Volcker, and four under Greenspan.

The data in columns 4, 5, and 6 of Table 1 were used to construct Table 2, which shows how well each of the four most recent Fed chairmen performed as custodian of the public purse.

During Burns's tenure, substantial technological innovation was brought into the Fed's operations, including the RCPC

216

program, to speed the collection of checks, the automating of Fedwire, and initiation of the ACH program. The average annual increase in Fed expenditures during his eight years was 10.8 percent, which was the highest among the four contemporary chairmen. After adjusting for inflation, the average annual increase was 3.6 percent, also the highest—and attributed to the Fed's investment in improved technology, which peaked during Burns's tenure.

Table 2
Performance of Fed Chairmen, 1970–2006

Tenure	Chairman	# Years	Average Annual Percent change in Net Fed Expenses	Average Annual Percent change in Net Fed Expenses
1970–1978	Bums	8	10.8	3.6
1978–1979	Miller	1.6	4.6	(2.1)
1979–1987	Volcker	8	7.9	2.1
1987–2006	Greenspan	18	5.23	2.17

Miller was Fed chairman for only seventeen months, and average annual expenses increased 4.6 percent, and a negative 2.1 percent, after adjustment for inflation. The Fed was preparing for its "packet switching network" initiative, which occurred during Volcker's tenure, although much of the planning had occurred under Miller. He was very supportive of applying improved technology to the Fed's operations.

During Volcker's eight-year span of leadership, Fed expenses increased at a rate of 7.9 percent annually and at 2.1 percent after inflation is taken into account. Volcker's most prominent contribution as Fed chairman can be seen in column 2 of Table 1, and his success in driving down inflation from its peak in the early 1980s.

When he left the Fed in 1987, inflation had been "tamed."

217

It increased somewhat in the early Greenspan years, but has been under control since 1992.

Greenspan's eighteen-year tenure as Fed chairman looks awfully good in Tables 1 and 2. Columns 2 and 3 of Table 1 show that price stability was preserved and employment was consistently retained at acceptable levels since he had assumed Fed leadership. Table 2 shows that he was attentive to controlling Fed expenditures, as these increased an average of 5.23 percent annually, the lowest among his contemporaries, and 2.17 percent after inflation adjustments.

Moreover, the Fed's operations were totally restructured under his leadership, creating a substantial economic benefit, as discussed in previous chapters. Improvements in its technological capability permitted the Fed to consolidate its operations and achieve considerable gains in efficiency.

At the time Greenspan left the Fed on January 31, 2006, he had already been "coronated" by all in our financial industry—as well as globally—as the greatest Fed chairman of all time. There were pats on the back for all of his colleagues on the FOMC, as well.

11

The Subprime Mortgage Mess

Within a year after Greenspan left the Fed, however, the subprime mortgage mess surfaced. When questioned about this problem, he initially stated that neither he, nor the others in the Fed, saw this coming. He followed this up with an article in the *Wall Street Journal,* in which he attributed the problem to the lack of sufficient risk management among the participants in the subprime scheme.

And of course he was totally correct in this assessment. But what he did not say was that when a financial industry just doesn't get it right, it's time for the regulator to step in and make things right. But then, you can't do that as a regulator if you are not aware that something is amiss.

The subprime problem cost him the top of the mountain among Fed chairmen. So let's review what occurred and why this mess materialized right under the noses of Greenspan's Fed, and, for about a year, under the noses of Bernanke's Fed as well, until it became a national problem known to all.

Instruments of Doom

Most of the residential mortgage loans that have become known as "subprime" were originated by the mortgage banking industry in the years from 2003 to early 2007. These loans were all originated without proper underwriting. Underwriting means that before a mortgage banker extends credit to the borrower for purchase of a home, he verifies that the borrower has the ability to make timely payments. Verifying the borrower's income, debt, credit history, employment, net worth, employment history, and credit ratings is included.

Moreover, many of the subprime loans were ARMs, meaning the interest rate changed on the loan periodically, usually every three years, and would go up or down, depending on the index used to reset the interest rate. Since Greenspan's Fed kept interest rates low for much of 2000 to 2005, the initial interest rate that the borrower had to pay on the ARM was low. This allowed the borrower to purchase a better house than he otherwise could afford. For example, if the amount borrowed was $300,000 and the initial interest rate was 3 percent, that meant that the borrower would be paying only $9,000 per year in interest payments for the first three years in the house. And since many of the ARMs originated were "interest-only" loans at the outset, the borrowers' monthly payment was a little over $700 per month, plus a monthly amount for prorated taxes. Subsequently, however, the interest rate could adjust upward by as much as 6 percent for the next three-year period. Then interest payments would go up to $27,000 per year, or over $2,000 per month, plus real-estate taxes. Such adjustments proved to be a problem for many borrowers.

Somehow, some in the mortgage banking industry believed that they could make residential mortgage loans without traditional underwriting. The advantages of this to the mortgage banker are obvious. More loans could be made in a shorter period of time, and since all borrowers pay certain fees, including origination fees to the mortgage banker, the more loans that could be originated, the more the fees that the mortgage banker could collect. The disadvantage is obvious: The borrower's ability to make timely payment is not verified up front.

The mortgage banker made the loans and aggregated these into a mortgage backed security, or a collateralized mortgage-obligation (CMO), or a collateralized debt obligation (CDO), which would then be sold to an investor in the market.

The mortgage banker was able to get the rating agencies, primarily Standard and Poor's and Moody's, to assign these securities their highest bond rating. Sometimes, the mortgage banker accomplished this by overcollateralizing the security—for example, including $50 million of loans in a security with a $40 million face value. Thus, if some of the underlying loans entered foreclosure because of nonpayment, the idea was that the excess amount of loans in the security would be sufficient to ensure that the investor would get his monthly interest and principal payments due him. Another way the mortgage banker could increase the credit rating on the security was to purchase insurance guaranteeing timely payment to the investor. The investor was purchasing a security with the highest bond rating applicable, and thus, presumably was protected against default.

Problems began to materialize when the ARMs loaded with subprimes began to reset upward in interest rates. Borrowers could not make timely payments as they no longer could afford the homes at these substantially higher monthly payments. More loans went into default in the security than anticipated, and thus the overcollateralization plan did not work. And the calls on the insurers guaranteeing principal and interest payments dissipated their capital because actual loan default rates were greater than those anticipated up front, bankrupting the insurers. The investors in the security were left holding the bag.

Ultimately the problem became widespread and was exacerbated by other factors, including a precipitous decrease in home values in markets that had had phenomenal gains in previous years, such as California, Arizona, Florida, and Nevada. Many subprime loans were originated in those markets. As the interest rates on those subprimes were ratcheting upward, the underlying house values were plummeting. The problem intensified when it became widely known that subprime loans were intermixed with prime loans in many mortgage-backed security originations, and that 15 percent of such originations in 2005, 2006, and early 2007 contained subprimes. This, in turn, created confusion and a lack of confidence in the market for any mortgage-backed security. The capital markets locked up in mid 2007, as there were no longer buyers of mortgage-backed securities, or sellers willing to accept such securities as collateral. Moreover, since bankers didn't know the magnitude of problems their colleagues may have had with their securities, there was an unwillingness to enter into financial transactions among participants in the capital markets. No financial institution was willing to accept any other financial institution's credit. The flow of liquidity dried up, and the markets ceased to function.

The Culprits

At the time the markets froze, our financial system was as close to armageddon as it is possible to get without actually falling over the edge. And these problems didn't materialize overnight. It took years of total mismanagement of risk at all levels in our financial industry to arrive at this nightmarish situation. Let' review the faulty decision-making that contributed to the creation of this monstrosity.

Clueless and Greedy Borrowers

Home buyers seeking residential mortgages were lulled into a feeling of euphoria by mortgage bankers peddling risk-laden instruments. Some of these buyers were just clueless as to what was occurring, while others greedily saw an opportunity to profit. Mortgages were offered that allowed home buyers to purchase homes they previously could not afford simply because the starting interest rates on adjustable mortgages were so low that they could afford temporarily to make the monthly house payment—but in many cases, just barely. Many did not focus on the fact that when the interest rate adjusted upward, as it was likely to do, the house payment would exceed their ability to pay. In some cases, the bankers calmed buyers' fears by telling them that they could always sell the house at a profit if that scenario should occur.

Predatory Lenders

The mortgage bankers, seeking the maximum profit from origination fees and securitization of the mortgages, abandoned traditional underwriting and took many shortcuts. This led to a proliferation of interest-only residential mortgage loans; loans in excess of 100 percent of home value; no-down-payment loans; loans made with partial, and in some cases, no underwriting; three-year ARMs with prohibitive interest-rate reset terms; and the invention of a new mortgage banking term, "subprime," as contrasted with traditional "prime" loans. The more mortgages that could be pumped through the system, the larger the banker's profits and bonuses.

The Rating Agencies

The enabler of all of this freewheeling in the mortgage banking industry was the group of rating agencies that somehow were able to justify assigning their highest bond rating, AAA, to the resultant mortgage-backed security or CMO or CDO into which these mortgages were loaded. Individually, these mortgages warranted a rating of somewhere on the "B" scale, or lower. But through the use of mirrors, sleight of hand, and other innovative ideas including overcollateralization and insurance, the rating agencies were able to justify, to their internal committees, the magical transformation of a bunch of B-rated stuff to AAA-rated stuff when consolidated into a security. Even our largest, and supposedly most sophisticated, financial organizations, including those on Wall Street, were flimflammed by such ratings. And so was the Fed.

Alan Greenspan, after leaving the Fed, said he believed

that the crux of the subprime problem was the misjudgments of the rating agencies. And this was an understatement because of the devastating role played by Moody's, Standard and Poor's, and the Fitches of the world.

Included among the risk-management procedures of financial institutions are the requirements for investment policies that are approved by their boards of directors and that govern their investment activity. Most institutions are not permitted to purchase a great deal of investments below an A-rated instrument, and can purchase only a limited amount of A-rated investments. The majority of their investments must carry an AA rating or better, and many require a great preponderance of AAA-rated investments. The simple fact is that without an AAA rating on their securitization of subprime mortgages, the mortgage bankers, such as Countrywide, would not have been able to sell the junk that they originated. And the subprime problem would have been averted.

How could the rating agencies have misjudged the ratings on these securities to the extent that they did? For decades, Standard and Poor's and Moody's provided ratings on organizations and their debt issuances that were relied upon by all participants in the financial markets. They did it well, conservatively, thoroughly, and accurately. I have dealt with them before, when I took U.S. Central Credit Union to Wall Street in the early 1980s to obtain commercial paper ratings. I know how careful they were in assessing U.S. Central, how knowledgeable their analysts were, and how thorough and professional their internal committees were in assigning ratings to us. What I observed and experienced then, and what occurred with the subprimes, just do not fit together.

Was it a case of the rating agencies accommodating the mortgage bankers because of the fees associated with this business?

Did the quality of the rating agencies' work deteriorate that dramatically to result in such grievous errors in ratings?

Was money passed not just for the rating service but to

"buy" the AAA rating on the security despite the underlying mortgages warranting a rating substantially lower?

The possibilities of what might have occurred are almost endless.

If our Congress wishes to get to the bottom of what really occurred with the subprimes, the place to start is the rating agencies. Interrogate the analysts who worked on the subprimes, as well as all of those at all review levels in the rating agencies. Bringing in the executives of such organizations for a one-day hearing, as was done, accomplishes little, if anything, of substance. In view of the terrible consequences of the subprime problem for our economy and for the global economy, it is inconceivable that Congress would let this pass without digging to the very bottom of the barrel to ascertain, with certainty, the cause or causes of such grievous errors in ratings. Sustaining our position as the world's financial capital, and our dollar as the world's currency, may be at risk if we do not.

The Fed's Failure

Similar types of issues arise when considering the Fed's complete failure to perform its regulatory responsibilities. And the place to start is at the New York Fed Bank, when Timothy Geithner was its president. The entire subprime mortgage-backed security mess occurred right in his backyard, better known as Wall Street, while he slumbered at his desk. That is where the investment bankers are located that securitized the subprime mortgages—Standard and Poor's, Moodys, and Fitch, which rated them, and Citibank and our other megabanks, which loaded up their balance sheets with them. Having been the executive in the Fed that oversaw Federal Reserve Bank operations, as well as evaluating the performance of each bank's top two executives, it is quite clear to me that Geithner and his bank were the Fed's first line of defense in the subprime mess. Their job was to keep very close tabs on what was going on in Wall Street at all times. (Geithner's responsibility in the Second Fed District, in this regard, was no different from that of any other Fed bank president in the other eleven Fed districts.) Wall Street is where our megabanks are concentrated, and the Fed keeps examiners in those banks permanently to effect close oversight. While these megabanks loaded up their balance sheets with toxic assets over a three to four year period, the mere fact that a concentration of assets of such magnitude was occurring should have raised questions even among the most inexperienced of examiners. But it didn't, even though Greenspan's Fed was directly responsible for creating our megabanks by permitting many mergers and acquisitions over his eighteen-year tenure, which greatly exacerbated the "too big to fail" problem. As the risks increased, the Fed's oversight should have tightened.

The situation was replicated in Washington, D.C. at Fed Headquarters. With all of those brilliant economists and lawyers, some of whom were supposed to be closely following developments in the residential mortgage market and reporting to the Board, and the Board's numerous committees, some of which had similar responsibilities, and a Fed chairman who prided himself on his penetrating analysis and his ability to discern financial trends before others, this thing built up to a crescendo, broke wide open, and no one noticed anything amiss until the horse was out of the barn and the only thing left was damage control. And that they did, to the tune of committing trillions of dollars to attempting to confine the problem and to flooding our financial markets with liquidity by expanding the Fed's balance sheet to levels previously not seen.

"This is the real problem. A large part of the financial industry, including banks and firms in the mortgage business, is highly leveraged and must fund their mortgaged-backed securities portfolios in the credit market, either by issuing commercial paper or by using their mortgage-backed securities as collateral for borrowings.

"Issuing commercial paper as a funding source dried up. Buyers of commercial paper demanded interest rates that exceeded the seller's earnings on their portfolios. You can't use a funding source that costs more than you are earning on your assets. Moreover, lenders were not accepting mortgage-backed securities portfolios as collateral. Essentially, the only liquidity available to fund mortgage-backed securities in the credit market was the Fed." (These two paragraphs are from "Credit Crunch Explained," *Kansas City Star*, Tuesday, August 28, 2007, James R. Kudlinski, guest columnist.)

But let's assume that the Fed noticed the problem materializing. Could they have done anything about it?

Not very likely. Or, at least, not until the problem became serious.

Can you imagine the Fed stepping in to take away from the consumer the subprime lending that put, within many people's reach, ownership of a home for the first time? During the buildup of the subprime problem, Congressman Frank and Senator Dodd, among others, extolled these innovations in mortgage banking. So, for that matter, did Fed Chairman Greenspan. If the Fed stepped in at that time to smother subprime lending, the consumer advocates, including Frank and Dodd, would have had a field day. Just like Congress and the Fed refused to regulate money market accounts over two decades ago during the S&L crisis, which would have taken away from consumers the high interest rates they were enjoying, Congress and the Fed were not likely to take away from consumers their first opportunity at home ownership. It would have taken a serious problem for them to act. But unfortunately, not the catastrophe that did occur.

Although almost three decades separate the occurrences of the S&L and subprime crises, the similarities between the two, and especially the consumer protection issues, are startling. These raise an important policy question. Can we continue to afford to make suboptimum decisions in formulating public policy and in regulation when the consumer may be harmed by the hard decisions required to ensure our nation's financial stability?

Other Financial Regulators

Issues similar to those discussed above also arise with respect to the failure of the other financial regulators, including the Comptroller of the Currency, FDIC, the Office of Thrift Supervision, the National Credit Union Administration, and the SEC to fulfill their regulatory and supervisory responsibilities. But it's harder to pin the blame on them than it is to do so on the Fed, the prime regulator in this mess. Nonetheless, organizations which they regulate also loaded up on subprime mortgage-backed securities, but not to the extend that the Fed's constituents did.

Although we didn't have a scarcity of regulators when this problem materialized—and we still do not, we have plenty—not one recognized the potential danger of what was occurring.

Finally, we should realize that the decisions of our legislators, particularly Congressman Frank and Senator Dodd, to support virtually any program that provided assistance to low-income home buyers contributed to the intensity of the subprime problem, and in particular, their encouragement to Fannie Mae and Freddie Mac to back riskier loans.

Greedy CEOs

The president of the Kansas City Fed, Thomas Hoenig, in a 2009 speech to a group in New York, said that there was a complete abdication of fiduciary duty among the CEOs of the large financial organizations in our country that were victimized by the subprimes. Simply stated, they abdicated their responsibilities to ensure safe and sound operations for their organizations, and so did their boards of directors. The motive was: bringing profits to the bottom line of the income statement, which triggered excessive compensatory rewards for all, but especially for the CEOs. These phantom profits were eventually eradicated after the realization set in that their greed turned into their worst nightmare, as outside auditors descended upon them and began to demand mark-to-market write-offs of a magnitude not seen on Wall Street since the Great Depression. These CEOs were supposed to be our most sophisticated financial managers, and it turned out they were anything but that. The things they missed are basic risk-management considerations.

First, never buy anything that you do not understand personally. These securities and CMOs and CDOs carried descriptions that were very complex and convoluted. In many cases, it was difficult to comprehend exactly what it was you were really buying, except that it was AAA rated. You didn't have to be a rocket scientist to question how mortgages rated in the B categories could be aggregated, overcollateralized, and/or insured, and materialize as an AAA-rated instrument. Based upon what occurred, it is doubtful that much analysis was done by the purchasers. It may have been a case of, "If it's good enough for, for example, Lehman, it's good enough for me." Richard Fuld, former CEO of Lehman, drove his 100-plus-year-old investment banking house into the ashes, but personally received as much as $480 million in compensation from 2000 to 2008, according to *USA Today,* December 17, 2008, "Who's to blame for the economy?"

Second, never ask what purchasing these assets could do for your firm. Ask instead, what is the worst thing that could happen to us if we make the purchase. If you do not fully understand the potential downside, you are not ready to buy.

Third, do not concentrate your assets in any one type of investment. Diversify, so if something does go wrong, it's not likely that everything will go wrong in a well-diversified, and carefully analyzed and selected, portfolio.

Fourth, obviously, do not rely on ratings. Do your own analysis.

I recall a similar incident while running the U.S. Central Credit Union in the 1980s, which had then had $15–20 billion in assets. We were, at the time, one of the largest sellers of Fed funds in the nation. Texas Commerce Bank, an "A"-rated bank, was on our approved list, as was the total amount of outstandings that we could have with them. Their rating suddenly changed to B+. I called in our staff, told them Texas Commerce was now off of our approved list, and that we were to cease doing business with them. I got some arguments from our staff as they stated, that B+ was still a good rating—which it was. But I told them until we understood why the rating went down one notch, we are out of there and will stay out. Subsequently the rating of Texas Commerce continued to fall, and it was closed by the regulator within six to eight months.

Even today, I still do not understand how all of these CEOs could all have made the same mistakes. Not one acted in a manner that indicated ensuring the safety and soundness of their organization was their personal and paramount responsibility, second to none. All of them walked away from the messes they created with compensation that was far beyond reasonableness.

Regulatory Reform

President Obama's Administration has proposed regulatory reform that should help to encourage better decision making in our financial system, including closing some regulatory gaps that currently exist that create huge liability traps and no oversight, such as in the derivatives market. But there are two additional areas that should be considered in that regulatory reform.

First, there seems to be little, if any, urgency among the executive and legislative branches of our government in nominating and approving candidates to fill vacancies in the Board of Governors of the Fed. Currently, for example, there are two vacancies, and in the past, there have been even more.

Because of how the Board does its business (as described in chapter 4), wherein the Board members are assigned by the Fed chairman to committees to oversee 83 percent of what the Fed does (the other 17 percent being monetary policy and directed by the Fed chairman), vacancies on the Board create real problems. The Board members that are there must take on additional responsibilities to cover the gaps created by the vacancies, and that is when the Board is most prone to potential errors and omissions. Remember, a full Board consists of six Board members and oversight of 83 percent of the responsibilities of the Fed is distributed to those members by the chairman. When two Board positions are vacant, that means that the work must be done with only two-thirds of required staffing. Take one-third of the workforce out of any organization, without decreasing the amount of work required, and what happens? And if the Obama Administration adds to the Board's responsibilities with it's proposed regulatory reforms, it will make matters worse.

Second, appointees to the Board have transitioned from multiple disciplines to a single discipline, economics. During Burns's tenure, for example, the Board members came from banking, manufacturing, business, mortgage banking, and economic backgrounds. Over time, economics became the discipline of choice when nominating Board members. Today, almost all Board members, and Fed Bank presidents are economists. We seem to emphasize the monetary policy responsibilities of the Fed—thus the transition to economists almost exclusively—even though this represents 17 percent of the Fed's workload. But the subprime mess emanated from the Fed's failing to perform its mortgage banking and regulatory and supervisory responsibilities—which are part of the 83 percent of the "other" things the Fed does and where backgrounds in other disciplines would be beneficial. It only makes sense to again consider multidisciplining for the Board.

12

Bernanke: Prognosis

Ben Bernanke was selected by the then President Bush to replace Greenspan as Fed chairman. He assumed the office on February 1, 2006, following Greenspan's retirement on January 31, 2006.

The Challenge

Bernanke "inherited" a Fed from Greenspan that had undergone revolutionary change, a large part of it occurring during his eighteen-year tenure as chairman. On February 1, 2006, the Fed appeared to be in its finest condition since its founding in 1913.

New Fed Bank and branch buildings were constructed to accommodate advancements in technology and growth, among other factors. The Fed's decision-making structure for operational matters was totally rebuilt. New technology was applied to the Fed's payments-mechanism functions, including check processing, wire transfer of funds and securities, and ACH, to achieve orders of magnitude improvements in efficiency, effectiveness, and security. The nation's payments mechanism began, meaningfully, to convert the inefficient paper-based transactions of checks and currency usage to much more efficient electronic payments. After years of Fed coaxing and jawboning, success finally began to materialize. As a result, Fed check-processing hubs in the nation have been reduced from fifty in the 1970s to forty-five in 2003, and to two today. And monetary policy had its most successful run ever—almost fourteen years of sustained high employment levels and low inflation, without any major gyrations or perturbations.

But then the subprime mess surfaced after Bernanke was in office about one year and it produced challenges previously only imagined. Bernanke was required to lead an embarrassed Fed to its biggest test since the Great Depression as central banker and "lender of last resort." The Fed has since committed trillions of dollars to reestablishing liquidity in the capital markets, offering financial institutions emergency loans to shore up their balance sheets, and to contain the damages wrought by the subprimes, including a recession that has globalized.

Added to Bernanke's job pressure is the concentration in banking that has occurred, emanating, in large measure, from the Greenspan Fed's regulatory approvals. Today, about 351 large first-tier bank holding companies, out of a total of 5,151, control 87 percent of all banking assets. These Fed actions have created our megabanks, the failure of any one of which could not be permitted because of the fallout that would settle upon our banking and financial industries. We saw that clearly demonstrated when our government did not hesitate to bail out our banking system with the TARP program.

Moreover, because of advancements in banking products, such as "sweeping" balances from checking accounts (requiring reserving) at the end of the day into higher-yielding money market accounts (with limited transactional capabilities, and thus not requiring reserving), the amount of reserves held with the Fed—prior to the subprime—dramatically decreased over the years to just $10.8 billion. Reserves, which originally were intended as a safety factor in banking, were all but eliminated by the Fed's regulatory actions in permitting the proliferation of these types of account arrangements. But the subprime mess has required the Fed to greatly expand its balance sheet in the provision of liquidity and other assistance. This has resulted in the amount of reserves temporarily ballooning to $800 billion.

Bernanke inherited a highly concentrated banking environment in which the Fed's responsibilities intensified dramatically with the subprime problem. As the nation's top banking supervisory and regulatory official, he must continue to ensure that safety and soundness prevail—which is no small task in this era of megabanks when failure of even one is not an alternative. And in the not too distant future, he will be required to dramatically shrink the Fed's swollen balance sheet—without triggering a recessionary relapse—and we must hope that the Fed's efforts in rekindling our economy through the provision of massive amounts of liquidity, and the government's stimulative fiscal policies, do not trigger inflationary pressures. That could launch us into a follow-up recessionary period as Bernanke would be required to raise interest rates to slow economic growth and ring out inflation.

Also contributing to Bernanke's challenges are the revolutionary changes occurring in our economy. Among these are a burgeoning deficit now being funded by foreign creditors, which makes everyone, including the FOMC and China, uncomfortable; high energy and oil prices, a likely harbinger of price instability; a growing balance-of-payments problem with no solution in sight; a softening dollar; and our rapid transition to a global economy. But the point to be made is that as time moves on and our economy becomes more complex, and as the rate of change therein accelerates, the orchestration of monetary policy has become substantially more difficult. And so have the Fed's other responsibilities, which many expect to be expanded through regulatory reform.

And let's not forget that the toxic assets are still on the balance sheets of our financial institutions, and that is another problem you can toss into the hat for Bernanke to deal with. (In this regard, the silence of the Obama Administration in even mentioning Treasury Secretary Geithner's plan to deal with the problem is deafening.)

So, how does Bernanke—selected by President Obama for a second term—rate on the job he has done to date as Fed chairman, and what can we expect from him in the future?

Monetary Policy

Bernanke possesses an outstanding academic and technical background for the lead role as our nation's chief monetary policy strategist. He has a Ph.D. in economics, and his specialty has been monetary-policy. His background is similar to that of Burns, who also was a college professor and on the President's Council of Economic Advisers prior to becoming Fed chairman.

But unlike Burns, Bernanke also was a member of the Board of Governors of the Federal Reserve System for a period of about three years, from August 2002 to April 2005, serving under Greenspan's leadership. This enabled him to become familiar and comfortable with the workings of the FOMC and its monetary-policy staff and resources. Having had the experience of working inside the Fed prior to becoming a Board member has indeed proven to be very beneficial. Those Board members that I worked with who had this advantage, including Mitchell, Holland, Coldwell, Gramley, and Partee, demonstrated the importance and usefulness of such experience after having assumed the office of Board member. No doubt, such "inside" experience also better prepares one for assuming the FOMC chairmanship, as Volcker amply demonstrated. Volcker was president of the New York Fed and vice chairman of the FOMC prior to assuming the Fed chairmanship.

After the then President Bush introduced Bernanke as his choice to replace Greenspan, the media began its speculation on what could be expected from him.

One story was reported that Bernanke would raise interest rates at the first FOMC meeting he chaired, which occurred in March, 2006, whether it was needed or not—just to show the world that he (Bernanke) would be as strong an inflation fighter as Greenspan. Although the FOMC did raise interest rates at that meeting, and at subsequent meetings, it was because of inflationary pressures, and not for Bernanke's image.

Another story reported that the Fed was interested in getting Greenspan to stop raising the Fed-funds rate at the last FOMC meeting that he chaired, so that Bernanke did not have to chair the meeting at which the Fed stops raising interest rates. According to the story, it would have been better to have Greenspan chair that meeting so that Bemanke did not appear "soft" on inflation. That did not occur.

Can you imagine Bernanke asking the FOMC membership to raise the Fed-funds rate just so that he could appear to be a tough inflation fighter, and for no other reason? Or for Greenspan to ask the FOMC members to turn off the interest rate increases—even though the data showed otherwise—just so Bernanke did not have to be the first to do so?

That is not how the FOMC operates, nor has it ever operated in such a manner. If indeed Bernanke and Greenspan did request such moves by the FOMC membership, they would end up on the minority side of the tally of the twelve votes. No FOMC chairman ever wants to be in that position.

Bernanke testified at his Senate confirmation hearings that he would continue with Greenspan's policies, and that he would go "slowly" when considering whether or not a numeric value should be published by the FOMC as its inflation target. This still has not been done. He was a proponent of the latter when he was a Board member, and Greenspan was against doing so.

Whether or not the FOMC under Bernanke ultimately decides to publish a numeric target will be dependent upon whether or not it believes the increased disclosure to the public is worth whatever such action would remove from the flexibility of the FOMC in orchestrating monetary policy. This additional element of information would be welcomed by the markets, but is not essential for their efficient functioning.

While a member of the Board and prior to becoming Fed chairman, Bernanke also was a proponent of increased disclosure by the FOMC in their communications to the market. He made known his desires to be more open and transparent in communicating, and this he has done, having already been more forthcoming than Greenspan was as chairman for eighteen years. The irony, however, is that Bernanke came across—in the opening months of his tenure—somewhat as a vacillating professor.

Shortly after suggesting to Congress that a pause in the FOMC's tightening actions may be appropriate, he delivered a hawkish speech to the International Monetary Conference, indicating further tightening actions were required, which totally confused the market. He then did an about face, and a short time later, in early June 2006, in a speech to the Economic Club of Chicago, indicated there were signs that inflationary pressures were abetting.

Moreover, he permitted far too many Fed people to make speeches implying the direction of further interest-rate movements, which added to the market's unrest and confusion. This prompted some on Wall Street to refer to his FOMC as the "Federal Open Mouth Committee." Bernanke, in his quest to be more open and transparent, thus appears to have opened the barn door and let some horses run loose. However, things tightened up, especially after the subprime problem surfaced.

By comparison, his predecessor, Greenspan, held everything close to the vest, carefully chose every word he spoke or wrote, and communicated only the barest essentials in obfuscated language. Many will recall Greenspan's response to a member of Congress while testifying on the Hill. When the legislator stated he understood what the Fed chairman was saying, Greenspan said that if he did, then he (Greenspan) must have misspoken. Greenspan was able to get away with not being forthcoming simply because his record as Fed chairman was so good, excluding the subprime problem.

At the outset of the subprime problems, Bernanke thought that the fallout could be contained and he publicly said so, and that was an error in his judgment. But since then, his actions in ameliorating the problem and its fallout have been consistent with the Fed's title of "lender of last resort." He has flooded the capital markets with liquidity and, as FOMC chairman, has lowered the Fed-funds rate effectively to zero. In view of the magnitude of problems our nation was and is now facing, including our worst recession since the Great Depression, such actions were right on. That is why we have a central banker. Bernanke proved his mettle for the job by not hesitating to act when delayed action could have created the onset of armageddon in the global economy.

The Rest of the Job

The "total" job of the Fed chairman incorporates the FOMC chairmanship as well as the CEO responsibilities for the other 83 percent of what the Fed does (as described in earlier chapters). And this is where a Fed chairman can get embarrassed, as did Greenspan by the subprime mess, and as Bernanke himself was tarnished. Bernanke's background has been substantially in academia, and more recently, as an economic advisor to the then President Bush while the subprime mess materialized, before he became Fed chairman.

His resume does not show that he has ever held a job with the scope of the overall responsibilities of this one. As the chairman of the FOMC, he has to motivate the other eleven voting members to accomplish his preferences on interest-rate movements. As the Fed chairman, and having CEO responsibilities for the rest of the Fed's operations, however, he has to motivate 20,000-plus employees, who are spread throughout the United States, to accomplish his objectives.

All of the media attention on the Fed chairman, and all of the notoriety that accompanies the position—once we get through subprime—will be focused solely on Bernanke as chairman of the FOMC and what he does with monetary policy. The rest of the job will be forgotten by the media until the next major problem surfaces. Only those inside the Fed, and its constituency of banks, savings and loans, mutual savings banks, credit unions, and certain portions of Wall Street will closely follow what he does with the rest of his Fed responsibilities.

When Bernanke took office on February 1, 2006, he instantly became a national and international personality. Suddenly, he was not able to turn on the TV or read a newspaper without hearing or seeing some reference made to him as our nation's chief monetary-policy strategist. In the past, this has caused some of his predecessors to delegate away these other responsibilities and pay little attention to formulating programs, leaving this to others, and instead immerse themselves in the high-profile area of monetary policy.

But a "hands-off" approach and reliance on others for all but monetary policy can be risky, and tarnish the overall reputation of a Fed chairman, as we saw happen to Greenspan. If Fed chairmen didn't have major egos, they never would have sought the job. The reward from the job is not financial gain, it's fame. When you get to be a regular on TV and in the media, it is captivating and is difficult to give up.

So what can Bernanke do to be an effective "total" Fed chairman, especially after subprime, given that his background seems to have prepared him for the FOMC chairmanship but provided little experience for the rest of the job?

He can replicate what has worked for his predecessors.

To be effective as a total Fed chairman will require strong leadership skills from Bernanke, such as those displayed by Burns and Volcker, and particularly under trying circumstances, like he has experienced with subprime.

To be effective will necessitate a thorough understanding of the importance of the Fed's payments mechanism and other operations, and of the critical need for revolutionary improvements as these become available through new technology. All of his predecessors going back to Burns, displayed this in various ways. Volcker was most knowledgeable because of his Fed Bank experience. And Greenspan was in the right place at the right time to benefit the most.

To be effective will require a "custodian of the public purse" attitude in controlling Fed expenditures. This was brought to the Fed chairman's job by Burns, but none did it better than Greenspan. Miller and Volcker also were good "custodians."

To be effective will require Bernanke to "demand" things at times, such as Burns did in 1975 in cutting the Fed's budget increase from 19 percent to 5.9 percent, and at other times to rely on developing a consensus. None was better at developing a consensus than Greenspan, although Miller also was adept at doing so.

Most importantly, Bernanke must become a good "delegator." Choosing the right leaders within the Fed, with the right backgrounds to manage key areas, and knowing when and how to follow up, are essential to the total Fed chairman's job. His three years as a Board member, and his experience as Fed chairman with the subprime problem, should have exposed him to how things get done in the Fed.

As described in earlier chapters, the Fed's structure necessitates reliance upon certain organizational entities to effect systemwide changes: The Board's committees, the Conference of Presidents, and the Conference of First Vice Presidents are the key entities. You get systemwide things done in the Fed through use of these groups.

And it all starts with the appointment of Board members to committees. If that is done well—meaning appointing Board members to committees that reflect their background and interests and maximize their experience—you end up with leaders who have a desire to leave their mark on the Fed. I have seen these types of Board members in action, and also those who became "caretakers" in their assigned areas of responsibility for lack of interest. George Mitchell, Jack Sheehan, and Phil Coldwell are good examples of those who left their mark. All worked for Burns, who paid a lot of attention to Board Committee assignments. I won't mention the caretakers, to avoid embarrassing them.

Although I didn't work with Greenspan, he no doubt had Board members working for him who desired to leave their mark—as did Volcker. Their records as Fed chairmen reflect this.

In the Presidents and First Vice Presidents Conferences, you get the same division. There are those who desire to leave their mark on the Fed—and Jim Mcintosh from Boston, and Ernie Baughman, Bruce Smith, and Dan Doyle from Chicago epitomized the "doers" in my era with the Board—and there were others who were caretakers. You don't get things done by relying on the latter.

If Bernanke, or any Fed chairman, gets this part of the job done well, subprime-type problems are not likely to arise on their watch.

The public approval ratings for the Fed have recently slipped to the thirty-percentile ranking because of subprime, which is as low as it has ever been since such surveys began. Hopefully, we will see these rise as the subprime mess and the recession become more distant memories. Public confidence in the Fed is essential to fully recover the power and might of our economy.

Postscript

George Mitchell passed away in 1997 at the age of 94. I last spoke to him when he was 92. He informed me that he was "out in the back chopping wood," when I called.

George was a robust man. Well into his eighties, he took stairs two at a time—often leaving others half his age out of breath when accompanying him.

He single-handedly led the Fed—some members with their feet dragging—out of the paper-based payments mechanism into the electronic age. I am not aware of anyone who did more with his time on the Board as a member, and later as vice chairman, than he did.

For fifteen years, his official public speeches focused on educating the banking industry, and the financial community, on the merits of electronic funds transfer.

And I never met a Fed person or a banker who didn't genuinely like and respect him.

George was right all along. He was the first to call it, and never even flinched when others had doubts: the electronic payments mechanism is here.

He was my mentor, my friend, and the best central banker I ever met.

To Jim Mcintosh, Tom Waage, Steve Gardner, Rolf Engler, and all of my former colleagues who are not with us anymore, thank you for the memories and your contributions.

To Jacqueline and her British husband, my very best wishes.

To Ron Kudlinski, my older brother; Ray Lemek, my brother-in-law and former all-pro NFL tackle; and Jerry

Kudlinski, my nephew, who are no longer with us, I could not write a book without you in it.

To my high school teammates who are no longer with us, including Joe Radzik, Tom Wodarski, Fran Deval, Jerry Cherney, Joe Gucwa, Ed Henzle, Bill Blazek. and John Majewski.

To my teammates on the Iowa State 1957 college baseball team that placed third in the nation and are no longer with us: Prentice Lamont (also my teammate on the ISU football team); Dick Bertell, starting Chicago Cubs catcher for eight years; and Tom Howard (also my teammate on the ISU football team). And "Cap" Timm, our baseball coach.

And to Joe Zubek, my summer baseball coach through grade school, high school, and college.

Bibliography

"Annual Report," 2000 through 2008, Board of Governors of the Federal Reserve System.

"Annual Report: Budget Review," 2006, Board of Governors of the Federal Reserve System.

"Annual Report: Budget Review," 2004, Board of Governors of the Federal Reserve System.

Federal Deposit Insurance Corporation, 1997. "The Savings and Loan Crisis and Its Relationship to Banking." In *History of the Eighties, Lessons for the Future: An Examination of the Banking Crises of the 1980s and Early 1990s,* Vol. 1. Federal Deposit Insurance Corporation..

The Federal Reserve System—Purposes and Functions, 1st ed. through 8th. Board of Governors of the Federal Reserve System.

Seidman, L. William. 1993. *Full Faith and Credit: The Great S&L Debacle and Other Washington Sagas.* Times Books.

Stanleaf, Dennis R., *Economics, Readings in Analysis and Policy,* Scott, Foresman and Co., 1969.

White, Lawrence J., *The S&L Debacle. Public Policy Lessons for Bank and Thrift Regulation.* Oxford University Press, 1991.

Index

Wallick, Henry, 24
Watergate, 32, 99
White House, 87, 88, 200, 204,
    208
Willes, Mark, 46

Williams, Jim, 159
Wilson, President Woodrow, 75
Winn, Willis, 77, 202
World Bank, 78
Wriston, Walter, 94